Fitness WALKING

FITNESS SPECTRUM SERIES

Therese Iknoian
Athlete and Fitness Educator

Human Kinetics

To my parents, who taught me to strive for the highest goal, who believed in me and my ambitions, and who always supported my dreams. I am grateful and fortunate to have such a cheering section.

Library of Congress Catalog Information

Iknoian, Therese, 1957-
  Fitness walking / Therese Iknoian.
    p.   cm. -- (Fitness spectrum series)
  Includes index.
  ISBN 0-87322-553-8
  1. Walking.   2. Physical fitness.   I. Title.   II. Series.
  GV502.I45 1995   94-32259
  613.7'176--dc20   CIP

ISBN: 0-87322-553-8

"Assessing Your Walking Fitness" on pp. 26-28 is from *Jog, Run, Race* (pp. 20-22) by J. Henderson, 1978, Mountain View, CA: Anderson World. Copyright 1978 by Joe Henderson. Adapted by permission.

Developmental Editor: Marni Basic; **Assistant Editors:** Jacqueline Blakley, Ed Giles, Susan Moore, and Julie Ohnemus; **Copyeditor:** Molly Bentsen; **Proofreader:** Karen Bojda; **Indexer:** Theresa J. Schaefer; **Typesetter:** Ruby Zimmerman; **Text Designer:** Keith Blomberg; **Layout:** Stuart Cartwright and Ruby Zimmerman; **Photo Editors:** Boyd LaFoon and Karen Maier; **Cover Designer:** Jack Davis, **Photographer (cover):** © John Huet; **Photographer (principal interior):** Chris Brown; **Models:** Sherri Bolen, Dawn Roselund, and Jeff Williams; **Illustrator:** Studio 2D; **Printer:** Paramount

Human Kinetics books are available at special discounts for bulk purchase. Special editions or book excerpts can also be created to specification. For details, contact the Special Sales Manager at Human Kinetics.

Printed in Hong Kong   10 9 8 7 6

Human Kinetics
Web site: www.HumanKinetics.com

United States: Human Kinetics
P.O. Box 5076
Champaign, IL 61825-5076
800-747-4457
e-mail: humank@hkusa.com

Canada: Human Kinetics
475 Devonshire Road, Unit 100
Windsor, ON N8Y 2L5
800-465-7301 (in Canada only)
e-mail: orders@hkcanada.com

Europe: Human Kinetics
107 Bradford Road
Stanningley
Leeds LS28 6AT, United Kingdom
+44 (0)113 255 5665
e-mail: hk@hkeurope.com

Australia: Human Kinetics
57A Price Avenue
Lower Mitcham, South Australia 5062
08 8277 1555
e-mail: liahka@senet.com.au

New Zealand: Human Kinetics
P.O. Box 105-231, Auckland Central
09-523-3462
e-mail: hkp@ihug.co.nz

Contents

Acknowledgments   iv

Part I   Preparing for a Walk   1

Chapter 1   Walking for Fitness   3
Chapter 2   Getting Equipped   13
Chapter 3   Checking Your Walking Fitness Level   25
Chapter 4   Walking the Right Way   33
Chapter 5   Warming Up and Cooling Down   41

Part II   Walking Workout Zones   49

Chapter 6   Green Zone   55
Chapter 7   Blue Zone   67
Chapter 8   Purple Zone   79
Chapter 9   Yellow Zone   91
Chapter 10   Orange Zone   103
Chapter 11   Red Zone   115

Part III   Training by the Workout Zones   129

Chapter 12   Setting Up Your Program   131
Chapter 13   Sample Walking Programs   137
Chapter 14   Cross-Training   147
Chapter 15   Charting Your Progress   153

Index   157

About the Author   161

Acknowledgments

Without realizing it, my walking students over the years have made vital contributions to this book. Without their endless questions, I would never have had the chance to fine-tune answers or my teaching style. Special thanks also go to Royal Courts Club Fitness in San Jose, where the management allowed me to teach a walking class years before fitness walking was accepted as viable exercise. That class—and its merry band of regulars, including Barry, Ursula, Jon, Joyce, Joe, and Peggy—helped convince me that walking is a great form of exercise for the masses, which also allows fun, play, and social time.

Editors at *The Walking Magazine*, too, have been instrumental in allowing me to write for walkers and about walking. To them goes my greatest appreciation. Nike, Inc., also earns my admiration for trying to educate people about walking and allowing me to develop its instructional program. Kris believed in me, allowed me creator's freedoms, and shared every laugh along the bumpy road.

Without my race walking "family," however, none of this would have jelled as it has. The Golden Gate Race Walkers and the USA Track & Field (both the Pacific Association and the National Race Walk Committee) work single-mindedly toward one end—showing the public that walking is a real workout at whatever level. I thank my GGRW family for mile after mile in rain and shine, as well as for countless postworkout breakfasts with laughs, commiserations, gossip, and lively discussions of technique and races. (Thanks also go to the members who graciously acted as models for many of this book's photographs.)

Extra-special thanks also go to my walking mentor, race walking pro, and best friend, Ron Daniel, for sticking by my side. He'll always be a champion to me.

All these special people—and the rest of my family and friends—have made it possible for me to answer short and simply to the question: "What are you up to these days?"

My answer? "Writing . . . walking . . . or writing about walking."

My thanks and bear hugs to all.

PART I

PREPARING FOR A WALK

For years we overlooked the obvious in our quest for the perfect exercise. We pulled, pushed, and pounded ourselves silly trying to find the shortest, fastest route to fitness and health.

And all this time, the vehicle was right at our feet: walking. How simple.

That's exactly why we overlooked it. It seems too simple, sometimes even to those already convinced of its merits. It doesn't hurt. Anyone, of any fitness level, can use it. We learned the basics as toddlers. We don't need any fandangled, expensive equipment. And the only membership required is a free one—to the great outdoors. This couldn't be enough to pump up our heart and lungs, help us lose fat and tone muscle, and give us the bounce in our step and zip in our life we all crave, could it?

It could, and it will. This book will show you how, no matter what your fitness level or previous walking expertise.

If you're thinking about taking up walking for the first time, I'll show you how to make sure you're ready to start a fitness program with some basic evaluations. The primer on walking technique will show you how to get started slowly and safely, building a program as your fitness increases.

Maybe you've tried walking but never felt you could raise your heart rate sufficiently to achieve fitness gains. For you, I'll present extra technique and workout tips to pick up the intensity of your walking routines.

If you've built some fitness in another activity but are new to walking, you'll learn how to assess your walking level and find out what walking workouts you should begin with.

If you're already a dedicated walker, you'll discover ways to fine-tune your skill, spice up your routine, and conquer new challenges. For those who want even greater challenge, I'll introduce race walking, the competitive art of walking seen in the Olympic Games—a sport that can be more physically demanding than running and more mentally demanding than chess.

For every reader, this book will be a road map for lifetime fitness. That's because walking fits any age, any ability, any body type, and any environment.

In Part I I'll get you pointed in the right direction, laying the foundation for step-by-step progress. I'll help you meet all these important objectives:

- Evaluate the merits of walking in comparison to other activities. (Look for information on benefits ranging from cardiovascular fitness to body composition changes.)
- Decide what to wear according to the weather, as well as how to choose the best shoe for your foot.
- Assess your current fitness level with easy self-tests. The results will help you decide what kind of walking workouts you're ready to tackle.
- Refine your walking technique to make sure you get the most from a workout at any level.
- Understand the best way to warm up and cool down and learn several stretches targeted for walkers' muscles.

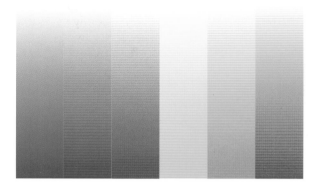

Walking for Fitness

As fitness boomed in the 1970s and '80s, walking was the slighted stepchild. Pooh-poohed as the activity of wimps and grandparents, walking wasn't even surveyed until the mid-1980s by the sports data gurus who monitor the annual growth of fitness activities. If you walked, you didn't admit it: "Going for a run?" more than one hotel clerk has asked me as I head out the door in tights and athletic shoes. I used to take the easy road in response—drop my eyes, nod affirmatively, and bolt for the door, even jogging a few steps to carry out the ruse. No more. Now I correct questioners with authority: "No, I'm going for a walk."

Who Walks?

Walking has grown tremendously since those days of hiding in the closet. More people walk—and proudly admit it—than participate in any other fitness activity across the United States. The National Sporting Goods Association counts some 70 million walkers, a number that grew by nearly 30 million between 1985 and 1990. (Of course, that figure includes anyone who's walked for exercise as few as six times in a year.) Some 14 million call walking their primary mode of exercise, hitting their stride at least 100 days a year, according to the Sporting Goods Manufacturers Association. That's nearly double the number of runners.

With that many hard-core walkers, it's not surprising that the sport now has its own national magazine, a slick, glossy reader called, simply, *The Walking Magazine*. Kicked off to skepticism in the publishing industry in 1986, the magazine quickly gained popularity. Circulation now hovers around a half million readers—young and old, women and men, racers and striders, proud walkers all. In 1993 the magazine sponsored a survey by American Sports Data. The results show that two thirds of walkers are women with a median age of 46. Men who walk have a median age of 54. All express a deep commitment to the activity.

The survey also discovered that dedicated walkers are getting younger, as more and more Americans realize they don't have to hurt to get fit. Most people who have been walking for a year or less are younger than 34. The credos of "No pain, no gain" and "Go for the burn" are dinosaurs in today's fitness world.

With that many walkers, the number of short races (5K, or kilometers, or 3.1 miles) and shorter walks added to 10K (6.2-mile) fun runs has skyrocketed since 1988, with corresponding increases in participants (according to the USA Track & Field Road Running Information Center). That's because race organizers have discovered that walkers are more inclined to sign up for shorter distance events, which they can finish more easily. Plus, walkers, like runners, want to be part of celebrations of fitness and camaraderie.

© Ken Lee

Anyone can find enjoyment and fitness in walking.

Why Walk?

There must be a reason all these folks are taking up walking. "It was the mid-1980s, and the running boom was over," says Brad Ketchum, who, as founding editor of *The Walking Magazine* for its first 6-1/2 years, watched readers grow with the sport's growth. "Americans were getting more fit and getting into low-impact aerobic exercise." With less inclination to pound the ground to stay fit, Ketchum says, one sport was left: "Li'l ol' walking."

Health researchers began taking a look at the nation's number 1 growing fitness activity. Soon, what the walkers intuitively knew all along was borne out scientifically. Regular walking will improve and maintain fitness.

Walking's Fitness Benefits

Let's take a look at how walking affects the five components of fitness.

- **Body composition.** Walking four times a week, 45 minutes each time, the average person can lose 18 pounds in a year with no change in diet, according to a study at the University of Massachusetts Medical School by director Dr. James Rippe. Walking can help you trim fat as well as tone your muscles.
- **Cardiovascular fitness.** Walking, at any level or speed, two or three times a week for at least 20 minutes increases cardiovascular strength. By increasing the strength of your heart and lungs, you increase your ability not only to exercise longer and harder but also to perform everyday tasks without tiring.
- **Flexibility.** As with any endurance activity, walking doesn't do a lot for your muscles' ability to stretch. Stretching exercises are vital to remaining free from injury. Every activity uses several muscle groups more than others. So if you don't stretch those muscles that walking works hard, they'll tighten up, stay tight, and perhaps cause pains or strains.

  Stretch after exercise, though, and you can stay loose. Chapter 5 shows you some flexibility exercises you can incorporate into your walking workouts.
- **Muscular endurance.** All walkers develop a moderate amount of endurance, which enables them to exercise for a longer time before getting exhausted. Race walkers have high endurance—comparable to that of marathon runners.
- **Muscular strength.** You will gain some muscular strength with walking, but not enough for well-rounded fitness. Muscles that get an extra workout in walking include the entire back of the leg, from the calves to the hamstrings to the gluteals in the buttocks. Take note that you'll also use upper body muscles in the back and shoulders because of the arm swing.

Walking-specific muscles become stronger, but their opposing muscle groups—for example, the quadriceps muscle in the front of the thigh, which opposes the hamstring muscles in the back of the leg—could get weaker and cause imbalances. Muscle imbalance can also lead to injury, so that's why it's important to do some sport-specific strengthening or choose additional activities that emphasize opposing muscle groups. I'll discuss proper cross-training choices in chapter 14 to help keep you moving and healthy.

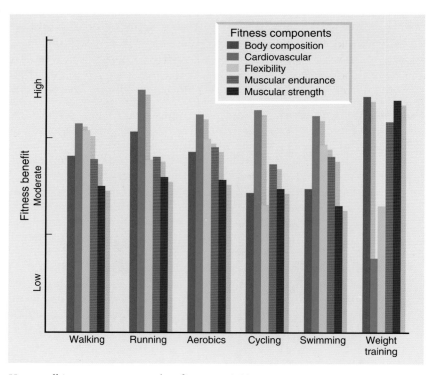

How walking compares to other fitness activities.

Other Physical Benefits

Of course, you'll gain other physical benefits too. Walking is low-impact exercise, which puts less strain on bones and tissues. Walkers land with 1 to 1-1/2 times their body weight per footstrike, compared with 3 to 4 times for running.

Weight-bearing exercise, such as walking, helps bones stay strong and dense, research seems to indicate. Although osteoporosis, a condition where bones become brittle, is a problem most common in older people, bone density can only be built and maintained while a person is younger.

Thin bones can lead to hip and spine fractures. A quarter of all women will ultimately fracture a hip, after which the average 6-month survival rate is worse than after a heart attack. Men aren't immune to thin bones, either; they just get them later in life than women do.

Exercise will help build your immune system, too. You'll get sick less often if you do moderate exercise. In one study by Dr. David Nieman at Appalachian State University in North Carolina, a group of women who walked 45 minutes a day were half as likely to catch colds or flus than an inactive group. This immunity-boosting response applies to everyone, not just women.

From casual exercisers to Olympic athletes, walking offers everyone a challenge. Walking can be a slow stroll as you get fit, a dawdling saunter to spend time with the kids or to recover from injury, or a high-level, challenging sport for both men and women. Or it may be all of these, according to your mood or your energy level.

© F-Stock/Caroline Wood

Share a few laughs with friends on a walk.

More Reasons to Walk

Walking offers other pluses that fall outside the scientific framework, but your soul knows they're there.

- **It's simple.** Although there are always various gadgets and high-tech shoes and clothing to tickle the fancy, all you need to walk is a pair of supportive shoes.

- **It travels well.** Whether you're at home, on vacation, or on a business trip, a walk is always just a step away. No need to worry about finding a certain environment (snow, water, smooth paths, hills, health clubs, aerobics classes) for a workout.
- **It's social.** Walks are a great excuse to spend time visiting with friends or catching up with the family. Whether grandparents or grandkids, everyone can join in.
- **It's private.** Walking is also a great way to be by yourself—to take some deep breaths, release stress, think through problems or happiness, or just relax.
- **It's efficient.** Once you learn to use your legs and pump your arms, walking exercises both upper body and lower body muscles. Many other activities rely on only one part of the body.

None of this is meant to say that you'll never have pains or strains because of walking. You'll just have fewer or will experience them less frequently or intensely.

ASSESSING YOUR PHYSICAL READINESS

Seven questions from the Physical Activity Readiness Questionnaire (PAR-Q) will help you assess your readiness to start walking for fitness. See chapter 3 for a further assessment of your health and fitness levels.

PAR-Q & YOU

	YES	NO
1. Has your doctor ever said that you have a heart condition *and* that you should only do physical activity recommended by a doctor?	___	___
2. Do you feel pain in your chest when you do physical activity?	___	___
3. In the past month, have you had chest pain when you were not doing physical activity?	___	___
4. Do you lose your balance because of dizziness or do you ever lose consciousness?	___	___
5. Do you have a bone or joint problem that could be made worse by a change in your physical activity?	___	___
6. Is your doctor currently prescribing drugs (for example, water pills) for your blood pressure or heart condition?	___	___
7. Do you know of *any other reason* why you should not do physical activity?	___	___

If you answer yes to any question, go no further until you receive a doctor's clearance. If you answer no to every question, you can be reasonably sure it's safe to increase your physical activity.

Walking Injury-Free

Walking is virtually an injury-free sport, but anyone who increases her or his activity level or tries a different technique or new workout regimen suddenly puts additional stress on a new part of the body or on previously unused muscles and tissues. It's possible in walking that you will aggravate an old injury that wasn't properly cared for, or you may discover a genetic deficiency or muscle imbalance that may have easily hid in your previous routine.

As with any activity, be smart, ease into each new level, and listen to your body. This book is here to help you along, showing you the pitfalls so you can dodge them and how to pace yourself as you progress. Although it is possible to walk every day without fear of overusing your muscles, a daily routine isn't one to dive into from day one.

The Walking Formula

You may have heard quite a few names for walking, and you've probably wondered if there's really a difference: power walking, striding, performance walking, aerobic walking, speed walking, fitness walking, sport striding, health walking, weight walking, rhythm walking—those are but a few. According to walking researcher Rippe from the University of Massachusetts, there are some 200 different names for walking! What a dilemma. Which type am I going to do? How do I decide? Am I an aerobic walker or a power walker? Do I want to be a strider?

Let's keep life simple. Walking is walking. Whether you're on your way to the car, heading around the block with the dog, or ready to do 4 miles on the local trail, it's all walking. You might go fast. You might go slow. Or you might go fast and slow. Maybe you add gadgets (I'll talk about the controversy over carrying weights in chapter 2). Maybe you walk up hills, along city streets, or around the local mall. Whatever you do, the technique is the same. Slight variations in arm position or foot placement only accommodate varying speeds.

The exception is race walking. When performed competitively, it is judged, and participants must follow two rules or risk disqualification. Those rules, plus the speeds attained by race walkers, mandate a special technique, which I'll discuss briefly in chapter 4.

For our purposes in this book, we can break walking down into four categories, based merely on speed:

- **Strolling** is a slow pace meant for beginners or for intermediate and advanced walkers doing an easy workout. Your heart rate will tease toward the low end of its training zone (another concept we'll get into in Part II). Still, this is more than a window-shopping pace. It can ease beginners into more vigorous walking.

- **Brisk walking** is moving fast enough to raise your heart rate into its training zone. This means different speeds for different people, depending on their fitness levels. It can satisfy all fitness and health needs.
- **Athletic walking** begins to incorporate a little race-walking technique so you can pump along at a faster clip, raising your heart rate to the middle or top of your training zone. This level might be perfect for someone who wants more challenges but doesn't want to bother with rules or take the step into competition. Athletic walking can also be used for speed play, where you alternate hard and easy periods in one workout.

© Ken Lee

Incorporate brisk walking for an enjoyable group workout.

- **Race walking** demands its own technique and usually involves competitive racing and a training schedule similar to that of competitive runners. The emphasis is on improving performance, against yourself and others. You don't have to *race* to race walk, but if you do compete, you must comply with rules, and you are judged.

Part II provides workouts primarily for the first three categories. Although this is not a book geared for race walkers, a beginning race walker could use the workouts in the Orange and Red zones to start some training.

No matter which of the four categories you think best describes the type of walking you want to do, Part III will show you how to combine the workouts into a variety of walking programs. Whatever your abilities and desires, you will improve your fitness, your health, your vigor, and your longevity.

Once you're immersed in a walking program, it's easy to become a disciple, preaching the joys of putting one foot in front of the other to everyone you meet. Walking offers a total package that's hard to beat. Now that you're ready to give it a try, let's start out on the right foot with some information about equipment.

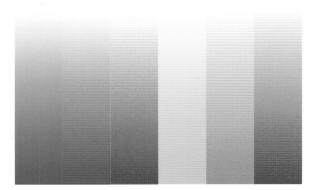

Getting Equipped

Walking's abundance of freedom and pleasure lies in its very deficiency—a deficiency in required equipment, clothing, and accessories. Every time I head out for a walk on an area trail, I watch the bicyclists and in-line skaters prepare themselves. They unload equipment, adjust gears and wheels, strap themselves in, buckle up, and pull on helmets and other gear. Although cycling and skating are fun activities, the preparation seems like an ordeal. Me, I just lace up my shoes, make sure I have on the right jacket or hat, then hit the trail or sidewalk.

In these next pages I'll discuss the walker's foundation—a pair of supportive shoes. You see, walking isn't just slow running. Biomechanically, the body moves differently when it walks and runs, placing stresses in different places, in different ways and degrees. Walkers require a walking shoe. Because shoes are all you really need for walking, I'll fill you in on how to choose them and take care of them, plus how to know when to replace them.

We'll also take a look at additional choices in clothing and accessories you might want to invest in as you get more involved.

Once you're outfitted, you head off to your free health club—the outdoors (or the local mall). Before you go, it's important to know how to assess and dress for all seasons and climates. Rules of the road and trail may be new to you, too, so I'll do a quick review of etiquette and safety.

Shoes Make the Walker

In walking you don't dress from head to toe, you dress from toe to head. Think of it this way: The snazziest, most finely tuned sports car on the road won't drive worth its salt without a solid set of tires. Your body, too, won't be able to reach its full walking potential without a great pair of shoes.

Walking-specific shoes are important for several reasons:

1. Walkers strike the ground hardest on the heel (rather than on the middle of the foot as most runners do), requiring good heel cushioning and stability.
2. A walker's forefoot flexes at nearly twice the angle of a runner's at pushoff from the rear, demanding more flexibility.
3. The high, flared heel typical of running shoes makes a walker less stable and acts as a fulcrum, causing the foot to slap down harder. That overworks the shin muscles, sparking shin and ankle pain. Lower profiles are better.
4. Walkers move in only a straight, forward motion, rendering useless the emphasis on lateral support in shoes for, say, racquet sports or aerobics.

© John Huet

Proper walking shoes help cushion and stabilize the foot on both the heelstrike and the pushoff.

What you need to look for in a good walking shoe, then, is a good heel cushion, a flexible forefoot, a roomy "toe box" so the toes can spread during the powerful pushoff, supportive heel construction for stability, and a low profile (a lower heel and less material under the forefoot). Faster walkers also want breathable mesh uppers so a hot foot can cool down quickly during and after a walk.

You can easily drop $120 on a high-end pair of walking shoes, but you can also get a good pair for $50. Any less than that and the shoe probably only looks the part and will break down or cause injury. *The Walking Magazine* and other fitness and general interest magazines do annual surveys of walking shoes. But don't take any rating as gospel. Every shoe and every foot is different, so go to a specialty athletic footwear store and try on all the name brands. A good store will let you take a quick jaunt down the sidewalk or hall, and its staff will even watch you move to see if the shoe is right for you.

If you plan to do many workouts on trails or hills, for better grip and stability consider off-road shoes—somewhat like hiking boots but still lightweight. Features might include a high top for ankle support, deeper tread for nonslip walking over dirt and rocks, and a higher heel to ease Achilles tendon tension while you're walking uphill.

If you're interested in race walking, you'll need special shoes designed for the sport's high speeds. They have extremely flat soles to better skim the ground and to accommodate the increased ankle flexion upon heelstrike, plus slipperlike forefoot flexibility.

Shoe know-how doesn't stop here. All shoes need a little TLC for good fit and wear.

Shoe Break-In

These days, shoes should be able to go from store shelf to workout without a hitch. Still, a new pair of shoes might pinch in a different place or cause you to land differently than you're accustomed to. Just the fact that the materials aren't broken down in your new pair will make them fit your feet differently. Try new shoes out on short or easy workouts to make sure they don't cause soreness or strain.

Shoe Wear

Your shoes might look great from the outside for years, but the insides lose about a third of their ability to support and absorb shock after 500 to 600 miles. For example, an average walker—someone putting in 3 miles three or four times a week—will need replacement shoes after about a year.

Be continually aware of how your feet and your body feel. More experienced walkers know a shoe is ready to trade in when they get a particular ache in the ankles or hips. Watch the tread to see where it's wearing out, and compare the two shoes' soles. Are they permanently tilted one way or the other (perhaps one more than the other) when you put them on a table and look at them from behind? That test will give you an idea of where your gait is uneven.

A potential knee pain might show up first in the wear on the bottom of that shoe! Shoes aren't the place to be chintzy. Retire the old ones to shopping trips or gardening, and keep your good walking shoes just for walking so they last longer.

Shoe Care

A few tips will help your investment last as long as possible. Don't put shoes by a heat source to dry because that will crack and weaken the materials. Remove the shoes' insoles after each walk so they can dry better. If you have two pairs, alternate them so each can fully dry between wearing, also prolonging their wear. After wearing your shoes, stuff them with wads of newspaper or bags of cedar shavings. Both help shoes keep their shape and soak up moisture and salts from sweat that break down materials.

Shoe Inserts

Few people have perfect feet. Most either supinate (roll outward) or, more commonly, pronate (roll inward). High or low arches might also demand extra attention. If you are plagued by injury, a foot malfunction might be the problem. Drug and sports stores sell a range of heel cushions, arch supports, and other inserts you can try. Podiatrists can measure your feet for personal orthotics, if needed.

Dressed for Walking Success

With good shoes on your feet, you're nearly ready to hit the road. A few other considerations will make your workouts more comfortable.

- The best clothing is made of high-tech synthetic materials that breathe and "wick" moisture away from your skin, keeping you cooler in hot weather and warmer in cold. But they can also be expensive. Natural fibers, such as cotton, are your next best bet, especially for indoor workouts where the elements aren't a big factor.
- Next to shoes, socks are your best friend. Avoid cotton there because synthetic fibers are better at drawing moisture away from your skin and they don't end up soggy. Wet socks rub and cause more blisters, too. Look for snug-fitting socks with as few seams to chafe as possible. For some blister-prone people, wearing two pairs of socks can eliminate rubbing.

© Ken Lee

Warm-weather walking demands proper gear for safety and comfort.

- Bottoms, from sweats to shorts, should be loose-fitting without bulky seams between your thighs to irritate or chafe. Consider long tights in the winter and thigh-length tights in the summer. Here, too, high-performance "wicking" fabrics are available, as are cotton, nylon, and blends with Lycra. Personal preference and budget will play the largest role in your decision.
- Tops, whether short- or long-sleeved, should also be comfortable, allowing freedom of arm swing.
- Headgear can both protect from sun in the summer and retain more body heat in the winter. If you're really worried about sun, consider a cap with a drape in the back to protect your neck or a hat with a wide brim.

- Hands, too, need protection in the cold. For cool days, lightweight glove liners are fine. Otherwise look for thermal mittens or handwear made of moisture-wicking materials.
- Cover up in the winter with wind- or waterproof shells and pants, preferably those that are also breathable to allow your sweat to evaporate. Layers work best—not only to trap your body heat, but to peel off as you heat up.

Trinkets, Toys, and Other Accessories

Walking's beauty is certainly its simplicity. Still, a few extra items or tubes stuffed in a bag can make you more comfortable. Your budding interest might also heed the call of an array of other helpful gadgets.

- Strange as it may seem, petroleum jelly is probably a walker's best friend. Spread a little on your inner thighs, under your arms, or between an elastic underwear strap and skin to prevent painful chafing.
- Sun protection is also important. Sunglasses reduce eye strain and eye damage. Use sunscreen, now made in thicker varieties that resist rubbing or wear, to protect knees, face, and neck.
- A digital watch will help you time your workouts. As you advance, you might consider a sports watch, with lap memory so you can time segments and track your progress.
- High-tech heart rate monitors aren't exclusively for competitors, runners or walkers, although they are more expensive. Whatever your fitness level, a monitor can accurately log your heart rate to help you stay where you belong for that day's workout.
- Personal stereos might be entertaining, but they can be dangerous, too—they can damage hearing and block out traffic noise or even the sounds of approaching dogs and people. It's best to leave yours at home, but if you really can't do without, keep the volume low or listen with one ear only.
- Carrying hand weights while running or walking has been debated by medical and exercise professionals for years. To make a long story short, dangling a pair from your fingers doesn't do much more than strain ligaments and muscles in your shoulders, elbows, and hands. Gripping weight can cause high blood pressure, too. And the increased calorie usage is insignificant. According to one Harvard doctor, carrying a 5-pound weight in each hand increased calories used on a 30-minute walk by a mere 5% (from approximately 200 calories to 210)—not much more than half a chocolate drop!

Adding Up the Costs

The cost of walking can range widely, depending on how extravagantly you decide to outfit yourself. Take a look at our low-budget tally compared to the high-budget one and make your choices accordingly.

Low-Budget Dressing

This list starts and ends with one item: shoes. Select a pair made specifically for walking. Shoes from major manufacturers (like Nike, Avia, Reebok, Saucony, Easy Spirit, Ryka, and Natural Sport) will wear better over the long haul. If you don't know how to judge whether a shoe fits properly, buy at least your first pair at a reputable athletic shoe store so someone with know-how can determine your needs. Later, to ease the

© Ken Lee

No need for fancy, expensive clothing—loose-fitting shirts and comfortable shorts will do.

cost, you might consider shopping at a discount store or outlet, where you can often find models for half the price.

Choose comfortable, loose T-shirts and sweats you already own. Wear your everyday watch, as long as your sweat won't gum up the works or ruin a leather band.

LOW-BUDGET COSTS	
WALKING SHOES, 1 PAIR	$50
TOTAL COST	$50

High-Budget Dressing

A walker's shopping spree can be just as expensive as any other athlete's. Find the newest shoes, and buy two pairs so you can alternate them. Select shorts and tights made of high-tech fabrics that dry quickly, wick moisture, and repel rain. Try tops, gloves, and even hats made to do the same. Indulge in a waterproof, windproof suit with a hood.

Go for all the accessories, like a fancy watch with memory and pacer, a heart rate monitor, upscale sunglasses, a sunproof hat with neck drape, and a waist belt with water bottle. The prices here certainly aren't top of the line. You could always spend more on anything.

HIGH-BUDGET COSTS	
WEATHERPROOF SUIT	$180
SHOES, 2 PAIRS	170
LONG-SLEEVE WINTER TOP	60
TIGHTS, ANKLE-LENGTH	30
TIGHTS, BICYCLE-LENGTH	25
SUN HAT WITH NECK DRAPE	30
SHORTS WITH LINER	20
MESH SUMMER SINGLET	20
WATERPROOF HAT	20
THERMAL WICKING GLOVES	15
TOTAL COST	$570

Creating a Positive Climate

Weather variations are what make any outdoor activity, including walking, more complicated and layers so important: They're easy to add when you're warming up or cooling down and easy to strip off when you're midway through your walk.

Cold climates can almost be easier to handle, unless of course snow and ice limit visibility and make footing precarious. In cold weather, try to pick a warmer part of the day for your workout and the warmest days for your harder walks. Cover the parts of your body most susceptible to frostbite (ears, nose, and fingertips). If you're particularly susceptible to the cold,

© Ken Lee

With proper clothing, you can walk outdoors all year.

carry an oxygen-activated heat pack for after your workout, as well as extra sweats. Get the sweaty, wet clothing off as soon as possible after your workout because the moisture will continue to draw heat from your cooling body. Be aware of the early signs of frostbite (tingling, numbness, or burning in the extremities) or hypothermia (pallor, mental confusion, or cold extremities).

Hot climates are always a challenge, particularly because humidity can make such a difference in effort and potential danger. Try wearing white clothing—that color reflects the hot sun better. Even lightweight, loose long-sleeved shirts can better reflect heat than bare arms. Try soaking a hat in water before wearing it, and punch some holes in it so your body heat can better escape. Drink plenty of water before and after your workout, and don't be afraid to sweat. Sweat acts as your body's natural evaporative air cooler. Stay alert for signs of heat exhaustion and heat-stroke: weak or rapid pulse, headache, dizziness, weakness, lack of sweating, and hot and dry skin.

Also, consider finding a mall or gym where you can walk indoors on extremely cold or hot days.

Heat-Humidity Readings

Keep the hot-weather ratings table below handy for hot days. Find the temperature on the left side of the scale and the relative humidity percentage on the top. Find where these two readings converge. A temperature below 75 degrees Fahrenheit is always safe (*A* ratings), and one above 95 degrees is always unsafe (*F* ratings), no matter what the humidity.Use good judgment when ratings fall from *B* to *D*. The typical advice is to exercise outdoors during cooler morning hours, but that doesn't necessarily hold true in humid climates. When it's warmer, such as in the late evening in humid areas, the air has a higher moisture-holding capacity, so the same amount of moisture in the air will result in a lower overall relative humidity.

Hot-Weather Ratings									
				Humidity					
Temp.	20%	30%	40%	50%	60%	70%	80%	90%	100%
75 °F (24 °C)	A	A	A	A	A	A	A	B	B
80 °F (26 °C)	A	A	A	B	B	C	C	D	D
85 °F (29 °C)	B	B	C	C	D	D	D	F	F
90 °F (32 °C)	C	C	D	D	D	F	F	F	F
95 °F (35 °C)	D	D	F	F	F	F	F	F	F

Cold-Weather Ratings									
	Temperature								
Wind reading	35 °F (1 °C)	30 °F (-1 °C)	25 °F (-3 °C)	20 °F (-6 °C)	15 °F (-8 °C)	10 °F (-10 °C)	5 °F (-12 °C)	0 °F (-15 °C)	-5 °F (-17 °C)	-10 °F (-19 °C)
Calm	A	A	A	B	B	B	B	C	C	C
10 mph	A	B	B	B	C	C	C	D	D	D
20 mph	B	B	C	C	C	D	D	D	F	F
30 mph	C	C	C	D	D	D	F	F	F	F
40 mph	C	C	D	D	D	F	F	F	F	F

Wind-Chill Readings

Keep the cold-weather ratings table above handy for windy winter days. Locate the day's wind speed on the left side of the scale and the temperature across the top. Find where these two readings converge. A temperature above 35 degrees Fahrenheit is always safe (*A* ratings), and one below −10 degrees is always unsafe (*F* ratings), no matter what the wind speed. Again, use good judgment when ratings fall from *B* to *D*.

Walks Happen

Walking for fitness is kind of a cheater's way of sightseeing. You can tour everything from your own city's neighborhoods to streets and villas in distant countries. Sure, paved trails and tracks can be a nice retreat, but they're unnecessary unless you're doing an advanced workout requiring timed paces and specific distances. Otherwise, anywhere that's safe is a walker's paradise.

My workouts while traveling are some of my favorites. Whether I'm on a tight business schedule or a relaxed tourist agenda, my walks let me gander around cities and countryside, finding sights, landmarks, off-the-beaten-track stores, and quaint gardens most visitors never see. Think of your walks while you're traveling as an exploratory treat, not an exercise chore.

Safety and etiquette rules apply no matter where you walk, especially if you're forced to share your turf with motorized vehicles:

Safety Considerations for Walking

1. **If you can't use bike paths or sidewalks, walk facing oncoming traffic. However, always walk on the outside of a blind curve.**

2. **Walk defensively. Don't assume the pedestrian right-of-way or challenge vehicles. Not every locale recognizes a pedestrian right-of-way.**

3. **Wear light-colored or reflectorized clothing at dusk, dawn, and night. Bright colors attract attention too. Or find tracks or other areas that are lit well at night.**

4. **Always carry identification with you in case of an accident or medical emergency. If you're traveling, carry the name of the hotel where you're staying.**

5. **If possible, walk with a companion. Otherwise, tell someone where you're going and when you expect to return.**

6. **On a path, stay to the right so faster walkers, runners, and cyclists or skaters can pass. Avoid "pack walking," which clogs trails.**

7. **On a track, stay in the outside lanes, unless you're doing a structured, timed workout.**

8. **Leave the personal stereo at home so you'll be alert to dangers, be they animal, human, or urban.**

Now you've got supportive shoes on your feet and appropriate clothing on your back, and you know where and when to walk. Let's take a look at your walking readiness before you set out to make great strides.

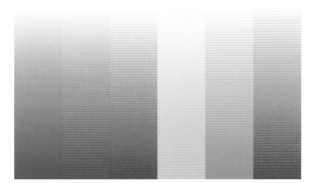

3

Checking Your Walking Fitness Level

Before you get started, it's important to determine not only how healthy and how fit you are, but also how fit you are specifically in the activity you want to begin.

You see, if you are a very fit cyclist, for example, you might not have the specific muscle strength or endurance to dive into the advanced walking workouts of the Orange or Red zones. On the other hand, if you have been inactive for a time, you may have developed some leg strength just from gardening or dog walking, and you might not have to start with the introductory workouts in the Green zone.

Remember, too, that healthy and fit don't always go hand in hand. You may be healthy in the medical sense (meaning you are free of clinical disease) but lack enough strength, flexibility, or endurance for physical activity. On the other hand, you might be strong from physical activity but show signs of disease.

So no matter what your health and fitness levels or your current level of activity, it's important to reassess them using the following evaluation. The key to a true assessment is to be straightforward in your answers.

Fibbing on an answer means cheating yourself and your potential. It could also lead to injury, rather than to maximum improvement and peak enjoyment of walking.

Test Your Health/Fitness

The PAR-Q basic health screening in chapter 1 is designed to set off alarm bells for high-risk conditions that need a doctor's consultation. It is only a general review.

The following is a self-evaluation that is more specific to walking. It takes a look at both your health history and your fitness background and level.

In each of the 10 areas, choose the number that best describes you. Then total the scores. The result tells you whether your baseline level is "high," "average," or "low."

ASSESSING YOUR WALKING FITNESS

Cardiovascular Health

Which of these statements best describes your cardiovascular condition? This is a critical safety check before you enter any vigorous activity. (*Warning:* If you have a cardiovascular disease history, start the walking programs in this book only after receiving clearance from your doctor—and then only with close supervision by a fitness instructor.)

No history of heart or circulatory problems	_____ (3)
Past ailments treated successfully	_____ (2)
Such problems exist but no treatment required	_____ (1)
Under medical care for cardiovascular illness	_____ (0)

Injuries

Which of these statements best describes your current injuries? This is a test of your musculoskeletal readiness to start a walking program. (*Warning:* If your injury is temporary, wait until it is cured before starting the program. If it is chronic, adjust the program to fit your limitations.)

No current injury problems	_____ (3)
Some pain in activity but not limited by it	_____ (2)
Level of activity limited by the injury	_____ (1)
Unable to do much strenuous training	_____ (0)

Illnesses

Which of these statements best describes your current illnesses? Certain temporary or chronic conditions will delay or disrupt your walking program. (See warning under "Injuries.")

No current illness problems _____ (3)

Some problem in activity but not limited by it _____ (2)

Level of activity limited by the illness _____ (1)

Unable to do much strenuous training _____ (0)

Age

In which of these age groups do you fall? In general, the younger you are, the less time you have spent slipping out of shape.

Age 20 or younger _____ (3)

Age 21 to 29 _____ (2)

Age 30 to 39 _____ (1)

Age 40 and older _____ (0)

Weight

Which of these ranges best describes how close you are to your own definition of ideal weight? Excess fat, which can be layered on thin people too, is a sign of unhealthy inactivity. Of course, being underweight isn't ideal either.

Within 2 pounds of your own ideal weight _____ (3)

Less than 10 pounds above or below your ideal _____ (2)

11 to 19 pounds above or below your ideal _____ (1)

20 or more pounds above or below your ideal _____ (0)

Resting Pulse Rate

Which of these ranges describes your current resting pulse rate, which is your pulse upon waking in the morning before getting out of bed? The heart of a fit person normally beats more slowly and efficiently than an unfit heart.

Below 60 beats per minute _____ (3)

61 to 69 beats per minute _____ (2)

70 to 79 beats per minute _____ (1)

80 or more beats per minute _____ (0)

(continued)

ASSESSING YOUR WALKING FITNESS *(continued)*

Smoking

Which of these statements describes your smoking history and current habits? Smoking is the major demon behind ill health that can be controlled.

Never a smoker	_____ (3)
Once a smoker, but quit	_____ (2)
An occasional, social smoker now	_____ (1)
A regular, heavy smoker now	_____ (0)

Most Recent Walk

Which of these statements best describes your walking within the last month? Your recent participation in a specific activity predicts best how you will do in the future.

Walked nonstop for more than 1 brisk mile	_____ (3)
Walked nonstop for half a mile to 1 mile	_____ (2)
Walked less than half a mile and took rests	_____ (1)
No recent walking of any distance	_____ (0)

Walking Background

Which of these statements best describes your walking history? Although fitness doesn't stick if you don't keep at it, if you once did an activity you'll pick it up again quicker.

Walked regularly within the last year	_____ (3)
Walked regularly 1 to 2 years ago	_____ (2)
Walked regularly more than 2 years ago	_____ (1)
Never walked regularly	_____ (0)

Related Activities

Which of these statements best describes your participation in other aerobic activities? Continuous activities such as running, cross-country skiing, and bicycling help build a good foundation for walking. Nonaerobic activities, such as weightlifting and stop-and-go sports like tennis, don't contribute as well.

Regularly practice continuous aerobic activity	_____ (3)
Sometimes practice continuous aerobic activity	_____ (2)
Practice nonaerobic or stop-and-go sports	_____ (1)
Not regularly active	_____ (0)
TOTAL SCORE	_____

A score of 20 points or more means you rate "high" in overall health and fitness for a beginning walker. You could probably already handle steady 4-mile walks at a brisk clip, 5 or 6 days a week.

Scoring between 10 and 19 points means your rating is "average." You'll need to start by walking fewer days, perhaps no more than 3 a week, covering a maximum of 2 to 3 miles each time.

A score of less than 10 points is "low." You'll probably need to start walking only very short distances, say around the block a few times. Feel free to take plenty of breaks, building to 1-1/2 to 2 miles of easy walks that you can comfortably complete before you try a more challenging program.

© Ken Lee

Testing your walking fitness can help you set up a program and gauge your progress.

Test Your Walking Fitness

Now comes the real test, the one that will reveal the most about your walking fitness level because you will be doing just that—walking. Paper evaluations are one thing. This is the real deal.

Based on a test developed at the Cooper Institute for Aerobics Research in Dallas, Texas, the 1-mile walking test translates well into evaluating general aerobic fitness levels for anyone 20 or older, of either gender and any body type. Simply put, you will walk 1 mile as fast as you can while timing yourself. You will use the time to assess your walking fitness level.

Although not a precise laboratory test that hooks you up to gadgets and tubes or results in an exact number that quantifies your ability to use oxygen (called "$\dot{V}O_2max$"), this evaluation will give you an excellent idea of how fit you are aerobically and how much walking you can do. It will also help you determine the structure of your future walking program.

One thing that might limit you during the test is a lack of walking technique, which we will cover in chapter 4. That's OK. Don't worry about finesse—just move as fast as you comfortably can.

Studies have shown that the biomechanical breakpoint between walking and running is a little slower than a 12-minute mile, or 4.8 to 4.9 mph. What that means is that most people's bodies will naturally tell them to start running when they near that speed. In fact, you have to use more muscle to continue to walk at that speed (or faster) than if you indeed broke into a trot. Using more muscle means you will also use more calories, by the way.

The test will also give you an idea of where your "lactate threshold" is. That's the point where your body can't provide enough oxygen fast enough to hard-working muscles. Without oxygen, your muscles can't get a proper supply of fuel quickly enough. Your brain hits the panic button, and that dumps waste products such as lactic acid into your system, which causes the burning, heavy, exhausted sensation in your body that forces you to slow down or stop.

The point where your body gets the cue to dump lactic acid is your lactate threshold. As you train harder, the threshold gets higher, meaning you'll be able to go faster and farther before being slowed down by lactic acid.

Enough of the scientific stuff. Let's walk.

The faster you covered 1 mile, the higher your walking fitness level. Note that I do specify *walking* fitness, because if you already exercise but you don't walk, you'll notice muscles after the test that you've never felt before. Even if you do walk but aren't used to pushing yourself for speed, you'll notice new muscles complaining.

1-MILE WALKING TEST

1. For an exact distance, use a school track or a measured and marked flat trail with a smooth surface. (A standard track is one-quarter mile, so you will walk four laps in the inside lane for the 1-mile evaluation.) Otherwise, use a measured path, a street you have driven to measure, or a treadmill.
2. Warm up for several minutes with easy walking and stretching.
3. Try to walk a pace that's steady but that feels as if you're pushing hard. Remember, you'll probably walk at least 10 to 12 minutes, so don't start too fast. Pick up the pace in the last couple of minutes if you still feel strong.
4. Your goal is to feel tired but not exhausted. You should feel slightly winded, but you should not be gasping and panting.
5. Continue to cool down by walking slowly for a few minutes.
6. Compare your time to the chart to assess your level.

Fitness category	Minutes for the 1-mile test	
	Male	*Female*
High fitness	<12:42	<13:42
Moderate fitness	12:42-15:38	13:42-16:40
Low fitness	>15:38	>16:40

Your time places you in one of three fitness levels, from low to high. No matter what level the test says you are, you can congratulate yourself for finishing. A low score only means you have lots of room for improvement, which you'll see very quickly as you start training. Plan to repeat the test occasionally so you can check your progress and measure whether you should change your workouts to accommodate improving walking fitness.

Taking the test is important because it helps you decide with realistic data where you should start with the workouts in Part II. Starting too low won't give you satisfactory gains, and starting too high will only frustrate you.

No matter what your walking fitness level, learning to walk correctly will help make your first steps efficient and motivating. That's where the next chapter comes in.

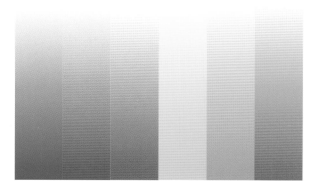

4

Walking the Right Way

Put simply, walking is just a series of forward falls. Keep falling forward, one foot after the other (without falling on your face) and you'll move along.

The catch is that walking technique becomes vital the more efficiently you want to move, the more you want to avoid some strains and pains, the faster you want to go, and the more you want to increase intensity.

Walking is not just slow-motion running, you see. Sure, we all learned the basics as toddlers—right foot, left foot, repeat as needed—but turning walking into a fitness activity demands a new dimension. Taking stock of how you move and adapting that movement to the technique tips that follow will turn your stride into a powerful strut.

No matter how fast or how far you go, standing tall is key. Hunching your shoulders forward tightens the chest and inhibits breathing. Dropping your chin to the ground does the same by shutting down your throat. Try this: Drop your chin to your chest, now talk to your feet. Pretty difficult, huh? Relax your shoulders and pull downward and backward with your shoulder blades. Tighten your abdominals, not only for additional toning but for good back support.

The saying normally goes "Take it from the top." Not when it comes to walking. Your bottom half is more important. So, let's take it from the bottom.

The Bottom Half

Large major muscles in your lower body power you along. Take advantage of that strength from hips to heels.

Heel-Toe

Compared to runners, who normally land more on the middle part of their feet, walkers should hit squarely on the heels with toes lifted high. That allows your ankle to move through its complete range of motion, from the heel landing in front of you at the beginning of the stride to the big toe pushing off in back of you at the end of it. If you aren't used to this action, you'll feel a burning or tension in your shins. Don't worry. That's only an underused lower leg muscle complaining.

© F-Stock/Caroline Wood

Be sure not to overstride when you step out for a walk.

The toes and foot of the leg behind you at the end of the stride offer major propulsion as you pick up speed. Think about trying to leave your heel on the ground behind you a split second longer than normal, and feel as if you're trying to push the ground away from you with the ball of your foot before your leg swings forward.

Stride

Overstriding can turn your walk into a bouncing gallop reminiscent of Groucho Marx's comedy gait. That wastes much-needed forward-moving energy. Avoid the natural tendency to take longer strides to go faster. That's what runners do. Walkers, on the other hand, need to move their feet faster by taking more steps per minute—"turnover," as it's called— while maintaining the natural stride length.

A walker doing a slower pace of 17- or 18-minute miles might take 115 to 120 steps per minute, while a typical brisk walk of 15-minute miles takes you up to about 135 steps per minute. A speedy 12-minute mile might mean 160 steps per minute. Notice how the number of times you "turn over" your feet per minute increases with your walking speed. But avoid short, choppy steps that can diminish your natural power.

Hips

Feel as if your leg actually starts at your waist. Extend the leg with each step from above your hip bone. That frees your pelvis to rotate forward with each leg so you can cover more ground without bouncing. Avoid excessive side-to-side motion, because that keeps your center of gravity from moving forward, which is of course where you want to go. Swinging side to side with the hips also wastes energy that you need to travel forward.

The Top Half

What goes on above the waist is the least of your worries at first. Only if you move faster does it become a concern.

The exception is your posture, which as I mentioned needs to be erect for everyone. Keep your chin tucked in, your ears over your shoulders, your eyes cast about 10 feet in front of you, your shoulders relaxed and pulled back, and your abdominals tightened.

Arm Bend

Are you imagining having to bend your elbows 90 degrees like the serious-looking walkers you see on the streets? You don't necessarily, if that's not comfortable, although most serious walkers do.

In two cases, though, the right-angle bend will help you. First, as you move faster, the long lever of an extended arm can't complete the swing as quickly. It actually hurts to pump it along while straight, and the straight arm will keep you from finding your potential speed. Second, if you experience swelling in your hands, bending your elbow will help keep blood and fluids from being pulled into your hands by gravity.

Arm Swing

Whether your arms are straight or bent, the pendulum action should start at your shoulder. If you use a bent arm, your elbow shouldn't move. Bending and unbending your elbow joint with each swing only puts extra strain on the ligaments and muscles and, again, wastes energy.

Also, control the bent-arm swing. It should be strong but remain compact to your body, with hands not swinging higher than the chest, elbows tucked into the waist, and fingertips not crossing over the midline of your body or reaching in front of you more than 10 to 12 inches.

Arms bent at the elbow and swinging close to the body help provide forward momentum.

Use your swing, powering it with your back muscles. Try to swing your arms faster, and your legs will likely mimic the speed. An added bonus is that the more you engage back muscles in the arm swing, the more you'll tone them.

Hands

No need to clench a fist. Imagine you're holding a fragile raw egg in each cupped palm—squeeze too hard and you'll break it, open too far and you'll drop it.

Race Walking: Extra Demands

You don't have to *race* to race walk. But if you do compete in judged races, two rules apply: The knee of the supporting leg must straighten for a split second as it passes underneath the body, and one foot must be on the ground at all times. Both are judged by the human eye.

© Ken Lee

A race walker's hip extension and hip rotation add strength and speed to a walk.

Race walking has been around for centuries. Men's race walking became part of modern-day Olympic Games in 1908, with competitors today testing their skills in 20- to 50-kilometer events, reaching speeds of 6- to 7-minute miles for the distance; women joined the Olympics in 1992 with a 10-kilometer race, in which many of them averaged 7-minute miles.

Race walking uses basic, strong walking technique, as I've just described, but it takes it a step further. The rear toe pushoff becomes almighty. Fast turnover means the difference between champions and runners-up. Arm thrusts from the large back muscles power racers forward.

Hip action, though, is what sets race walkers apart. Take a closer look at a good walker. The hip roll is really simply a strong fitness walker's hip movement (also described earlier) exaggerated greatly. It is not a side-to-side sashay. Any movement side to side detracts from the energy demanded of any walker to push forward. The hip movement allows a walker to cover more ground per stride without bouncing, and the more ground you can cover with each step, the more quickly you reach the finish line!

Good race walkers should look as if they're skimming the ground, nearly floating over its surface, and their heads should not change planes.

Knees, as the rules state, must straighten. Note the word is straighten, not lock. Locking the knees can harm cushioning cartilage.

Common Walking Errors

Everybody moves differently, but there are three common mistakes found among walkers of all levels, from strollers to racers. Guard against them, because they will inhibit your style or cause injuries.

Waist Lean

If you have an ache in your lower back after a walk, you may be tilting forward and letting your buttocks stick out. Stand with your back against a wall. Now lean forward slightly from your ankles. That's the proper forward lean. Now lean forward, leaving your buttocks against the wall. This is not the position you want to feel while walking.

Overstriding

Does your hair or hat or a scarf flop up and down when you walk? The way to eliminate the bounce and skim the ground usually means slightly shortening the stride. Every time your heel hits the ground in a stride that's too long, you're braking the forward motion. Experiment with different lengths. Try a really long one, then a teeny short one, then somewhere in between. Find the equilibrium where you don't bounce.

Elbow Whipping

The arm swing comes from the shoulder, not the elbow. You should imagine hitting something in front of you with your hands. Try this experiment: Put a long piece of string around your neck and hold an end in each hand, making sure your elbows are bent 90 degrees. Now walk. If you feel the string sliding back and forth behind your neck, that means you're swinging from the elbows, pulling the string down to the right, then down to the left. Eliminating the string burn will eliminate the elbow whipping.

Graceful, ground-skimming, invigorating walking requires learning some specific technique, but it always helps to make sure your muscles and joints are warmed up and loosened before a walk and cooled down and stretched properly afterward. That's what we'll cover next.

5

Warming Up and Cooling Down

People sometimes talk about "warm-up stretches." Actually, there's no such thing. There's a warm-up, and there are stretches. A warm-up should come first. Both are important when done at the right time, but the two in one breath contradict each other. The deepest of stretches—ones aiming for improvements in flexibility and not just loosening—come after your workout as part of the cool-down.

Warming Up Heart, Mind, and Muscles

When you begin a workout, every part of you needs to be eased into it—certainly your muscles, but also your heart and your mind.

A muscle after a day at work or a night's sleep is like cold taffy: Bend it, and it cracks, splinters, or snaps. When it's warm, it's soft and pliable.

A warm-up prepares your muscles for the activity to come, letting you rehearse in slow motion the way they'll move later. That means a warm-up for a walking workout can simply be walking slowly for about 5 minutes.

Your heart is a muscle, too, and it needs to be warmed up. Those first 5 minutes of easy walking coax it into working a little harder. You wouldn't start your car's engine after it has sat in the cold overnight, throw the pedal to the metal, and roar down the street. You know that you have to give the engine a few minutes to warm up, allowing all the fluids and gears to move freely as you slowly pick up speed. The same goes for your body's engine, the heart.

Then there's your mind, an important element to workout success. When you crawl out of bed or away from your desk after 8 hours, you probably don't feel like exercising vigorously, or even moderately. Promise yourself at least 5 minutes. Give yourself permission to quit after 5 minutes if you don't feel like going on. Most likely, those first few minutes will change your mind, convincing you the workout will feel good, and you'll keep going.

The warm-up also lets you tune in to any part of your body that's been twinging or aching a bit. If that part still hurts after the warm-up, take a cue and perhaps skip this workout. If it's not so bad after all, continue the workout but perhaps not so intensely. Listen to your body.

While you're striding through the "active warm-up"—the easy movement that comes before the stretches—take the time to roll your shoulders forward and backward, lift them to your ears and pull them down, drop your chin to your chest, move your head from side to side, and flex your hands.

Next, especially for more intense walks, take a few minutes for some light stretches to loosen your muscles. For less intense walks in the first few workout zones, stretches after the warm-up are optional. Remember, the deep stretching happens after your workout. Muscle loosening before activity can include some of the same stretches you'll do later, but don't push the stretch to the point of tension I'll describe in the next section. There should be no pain or discomfort.

Cooling Down and Stretching Out

Avoid coming to a dead stop after a workout. Just as you had to allow your heart, mind, and muscles to get used to the idea that you were picking up the pace, you have to give them the same chance to realize you're slowing down.

A cool-down is exactly what it says: cooling down your body after heating it up during a workout. Don't just jump into your car or a shower. Let your system cool off and return gradually to a steady state. Repeat what you did in the warm-up. Walk slowly for 3 to 5 minutes (or more if the workout was long and very intense), rolling your shoulders and shaking out your hands. Now you're ready to stretch deeply.

Muscles shorten as they tire during exercise. Stretching after a workout will return them to their preworkout length and perhaps teach them to be a little more flexible. Working out without stretching starts the snowball effect: You don't stretch because you're tight, but the more you don't stretch, the tighter you get!

Tightness isn't only uncomfortable. A tight muscle is usually a weak muscle, and tightness and weakness set you up for strains and other injuries.

After a workout, your muscles are pliable and ready to be stretched without getting hurt. Follow three easy rules when you stretch:

1. Stretch until you feel tension, not pain. Hold the stretch at this point and breathe deeply.
2. Don't bounce. Bouncing causes the muscles to protect themselves from overstretching by tightening. Yes, you'll actually be tightening your muscles if you stretch by bouncing.
3. Hold each stretch for 10 to 30 seconds to let the muscle relax. Continue to breathe deeply, and as the muscle releases, you'll be able to stretch a bit farther.

The following stretches will help you loosen up before and after your walks.

Hamstrings

Stand about 2 feet away from a bench or raised surface. Place your right leg on the bench, allowing your left leg to bend slightly. With your hands resting on your right thigh, lean forward, bending at the hips and keeping your spine extended without hunching. Repeat on the other side.

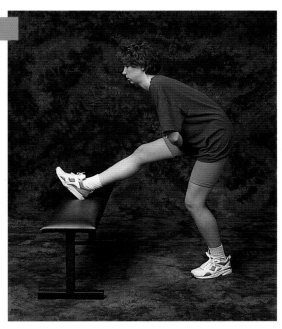

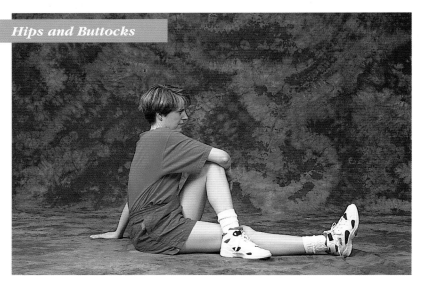

Sit on the ground with your legs extended forward. Cross your left leg over your right knee, resting on your left arm for support. Press your right arm against the outside of your left leg, pulling the knee gently toward you as you twist your head and torso in the direction of your left arm. Repeat on the opposite side.

Sit on the ground with your knees bent and the soles of your feet together. Grasp your ankles and lean forward, keeping your back straight as you stretch.

Iliotibial Band

Stand next to a wall about an arm's length away. Using your arm to support you, cross the leg farthest from the wall over the leg nearest the wall. Push your hip toward the wall, keeping the leg nearest the wall straight while allowing the crossed leg to bend. Allow your arm to bend as you stretch. Repeat on the opposite side.

Quadriceps

Stand with your left hand against a flat surface for balance and support. Bend your right leg behind you, grasping the ankle with your right hand. Bend your left leg slightly and push your left foot into your hand while keeping the knee pointed toward the ground and your hips pressed forward. Repeat on the opposite side. Avoid this stretch if you have bad knees.

Shins

Place the top of the foot on the ground and press your ankle toward the ground, allowing your knee to bend as you stretch. Repeat on the opposite side.

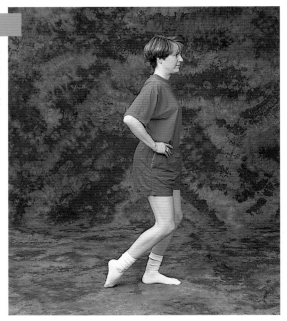

Calves

Face a vertical surface or object with your legs staggered; the leg farthest from the surface should be at least 2 feet away and remain straight, while the leg closest to the wall should be bent at the knee. Place your hands against the surface, then bend your arms as you lean toward the wall, keeping your back straight. Repeat on opposite side.

Back

Stand about 18 inches away from a wall or flat surface with your feet parallel to it. Turn toward the wall and place both hands on it at about chest height. Gently continue turning toward the wall. Repeat on the opposite side.

Lower Back

Lie flat on your back. Bend your knees and bring them toward your chest while grasping behind your thighs. Pull your knees toward your shoulders until your hips come off the ground. After holding the stretch, extend your legs slowly, one at a time.

Shoulders

Stand with your back to the wall. Reach back and place one of your palms on the wall with your wrist facing out and your arm outstretched. Gently turn your head and chest away from the wall. Repeat on the opposite side.

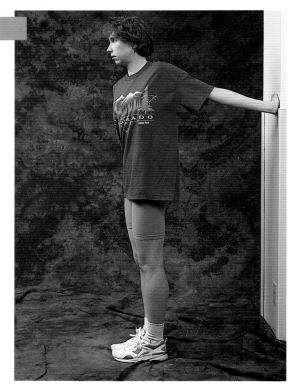

You're done reading about walking for now. You're ready to warm up, cool down, and stretch correctly—all with the right attitude in mind. Now's the time to charge right into the recommended workouts tailored to your needs and level.

PART II

WALKING
WORKOUT ZONES

Here's where you'll discover what makes this book special. Workouts are arranged by color, based on intensity and duration. That makes it easy for you to choose your workouts, mix and match zones, and keep track of your progress.

Green is the easiest, then comes Blue. Both are geared toward beginning walkers, as well as walkers at other levels who want an active rest day or something mild in intensity.

Purple and Yellow zones are for more intermediate walkers—those who need a bit more of a challenge—not to mention beginners who are ready to try another level or advanced walkers mixing up their program's intensity.

By the time you get to Orange, the level is fairly advanced. Red workouts are for the serious speed walker, perhaps someone who even wants to race. Intermediates may also try a few of these workouts for variety as their fitness levels adapt. Beginning walkers will need some conditioning before they can safely attempt one of these.

WORKOUT COLOR ZONES			
Zone (chapter)	Type of workout	RPE/ % max HR	Time
Green (6)	Low intensity, short duration	1-3/55-69	<30 min
Blue (7)	Low intensity, long duration	1-3/55-69	>30 min
Purple (8)	Moderate intensity, short duration	4-5/70-79	<35 min
Yellow (9)	Moderate intensity, long duration	4-5/70-79	>35 min
Orange (10)	High intensity, short duration	6-8/80-94	<45 min
Red (11)	High intensity, long duration	6-8/80-94	>45 min

Workouts also progress in intensity within each zone. The first ones are the easiest, building gradually to the last in each zone, which is the most demanding. Intensity is calculated based on a percentage of your maximum heart rate. In the easiest workouts, that might mean you'll exercise between 55% and 69% of your maximum heart rate. In the intermediate zones, some workouts will pick you up to a brisk 75% or more. In the superadvanced Red zone, heart rates reaching a tough 85% or 90% of maximum aren't uncommon. Note that a more difficult workout might mean you'll walk longer at a lower level or add hills, not only that you'll walk harder.

For variety, I've included one workout in every zone on a treadmill for those days when you end up in a health club, don't want to go out in the cold or rain, or are staying in a hotel and it's more convenient to go to the workout room. These are geared to be midintensity workouts for the zone they represent, but they can become higher or lower. Just take note of comments and modify the workout to your needs.

Maximum Heart Rate

Calculate your maximum heart rate using the simplified method: If you're a man, subtract your age from 220.

$$220 - age = max HR$$

Then multiply your chosen goal or intensity by the result. For example, a 40-year-old man who will be doing a Purple workout would follow this formula:

$$220 - 40 = 180 \text{ (max HR)}$$

$$\times\ \underline{70\%}\ \text{(lower end of}$$
$$\underline{126} \quad \text{Purple range)}$$

$$180$$
$$\times\ \underline{79\%}\ \text{(upper end of}$$
$$\underline{142} \quad \text{Purple range)}$$

Therefore, his target heart rate range for Purple workouts is 126 to 142, with the exact target depending on the workout selected.

Women use a similar formula, substituting 226 for 220.

$$226 - age = max\ HR$$

Then multiply your chosen goal or intensity by the result. For example, a 30-year-old woman who intends to do a Yellow zone walk would follow this equation:

$$226 - 30 = 196 \text{ (max HR)}$$

$$\times\ \underline{70\%}\ \text{(lower end of}$$
$$\underline{137} \quad \text{Yellow range)}$$

$$196$$
$$\times\ \underline{79\%}\ \text{(upper end of}$$
$$\underline{155} \quad \text{Yellow range)}$$

This woman's target heart rate range for Yellow workouts is 137 to 155, with the exact target depending on the workout selected.

This calculation is only an estimate; individuals can vary greatly. As you gain experience, learn to pay more attention to how you feel—your perceived exertion—than to your heart rate as you estimate how hard you're working.

Perceived Exertion

As you become accustomed to walking workouts, it'll be time to learn to read your personal "perceived exertion" level, which is another way to measure how hard you're working without stopping to take a heart rate. Learning to feel your exertion and to rate yourself means, as you've heard before, listening to your body. Our bodies are pretty smart, if only we'd tune in more often to the messages.

The rating of perceived exertion (RPE) scale, developed by Dr. Gunnar Borg, can help you gauge how hard you're working. Borg found that a person's sense of effort corresponds well to objective measurements such as percentages of maximum heart rate. On the 10-point scale, 0 is nothing at all, 0.5 is very, very light, 1 is very light, 2 is light, 3 is moderate, 4 is somewhat heavy, 5 is heavy, 7 is very heavy, and 10 is very, very heavy. An RPE of 1 to 3 has a corresponding heart rate of 55% to 69% of the maximum. A score of 4 to 5 has a corresponding heart rate of 70% to 79% of the maximum. A score of 6 to 8 has a corresponding heart rate of 80% to 95% of the maximum. Once highly trained, athletes can do short, intense workouts that push them to 10.

Caloric Cost

You will notice that as the workouts progress in intensity or length, the number of calories used also goes up. Even if weight loss is one of your fitness goals, be careful not to overdo your workouts with the goal to use more calories more quickly. Overloading your system too soon, at whatever level, can cause it to break down. With exercise, that means strains and pains that might put a stop not only to good exercise intentions but also to any safe, gradual weight loss. Heed the tortoise's wisdom: Slow and steady wins the race.

The number of calories you burn in a workout is the least of your worries, because it's usually not a huge amount. What counts is (1) teaching your system to use fat more efficiently as fuel all of the time, which will decrease your body fat, and (2) building muscle in place of fat, because muscle burns more calories than fat even at rest. That means you'll be using more calories just sitting in your car, for example, once you're more fit!

Be warned, too, that calorie expenditures vary greatly from person to person based on the metabolism you were born with; your muscle mass, fat mass, and fitness level; and how hard you complete each workout, as well as terrain and weather. The estimates in the table below are based on a 150-pound person. Add 15% to the totals for every 25 pounds over 150, and subtract 15% from the totals for every 25 pounds under 150.

Caloric Costs of Walking			
Zone	**Cal/min used**	**Workout length**	**Total cals used**
Green	2-3	<30 min	<100
Blue	4	>30 min	>100
Purple	5	<35 min	<200
Yellow	6	>35 min	>200
Orange	7	<45 min	<350
Red	9+	>45 min	>400

How Far Did I Go?

Many cities have trails that are marked every quarter- or half-mile or every mile. These make setting up a walking routine pretty easy. Otherwise, drive alongside your sidewalk route (remember, this is a rough estimate) or buy an inexpensive pedometer that will clock your distance.

You can also do shorter walks on a quarter-mile school track. Once you get the feel of how fast you cover a certain distance, you can use time as your guide to distance (for example, walk 15 minutes one way, then 15 minutes back for a 2-mile round trip at a 4-mph pace). Note that four laps around a track *on the inside lane* is one mile; for every lane outside that, you're adding a short distance. In the outside lane, four laps equals about 1-1/8 miles.

Pay attention to etiquette when you use a track. The inside two lanes are reserved for serious runners and walkers doing specific timed workouts (intervals) geared toward higher performance. Unless you need to time every lap you walk, fitness walkers and joggers belong in the outside lanes.

One more way to gauge your pace and distance is by counting how many steps you take per minute. Use the table below as a guide. Remember, this too is only an estimate because stride lengths vary.

Estimating Your Pace With Steps per Minute		
Steps/minute	**Mph**	**Minutes/mile**
60-80	2-2.4	25-30
85-95	2.5-2.9	21-24
100-115	3-3.3	18-20
120-125	3.4-3.6	16-1/2-17-1/2
130-135	3.8-4	15-16
140-145	4.3-4.6	13-14
150-155	4.6-4.8	12-1/2-13
160-165	5-5.2	11-1/2-12
170+	>5.5	<11

Last Words

Here's where we plunge right in to the walking workouts, five dozen waiting for your exploration. Each zone will introduce and describe its specific walks and needs. Don't forget to do the warm-ups and cool-downs incorporated into each workout. They're important for safe exercise. Once you are familiar with the workouts, feel free to adapt the speeds to your own tastes or needs. Focus on how hard you're working, not on how fast you're walking.

Be sure to read the comments with each workout, too. They will give you a few extra tips, instructions, modifications, or warnings.

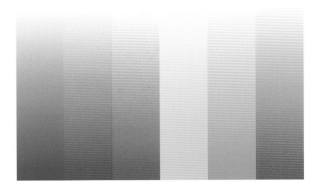

Green Zone

Green workouts are the easiest in both intensity and length. Still, they can be useful to many levels of walkers, although the pure neophyte to exercise will find them most useful. If you are overweight or have been inactive for a few years, you can certainly start with the Green workouts. The same is true if you've been injured and need a slower gear for a while. And even intermediate to advanced walkers can benefit from the easier workouts by sprinkling them in after hard workouts or using them during vacations to stay in shape.

As short sessions, Green zone workouts fit easily into coffee breaks and lunch hours. Because they're low intensity, you might not sweat very much, making it easier to get back to your desk quickly from a noontime jaunt.

Throughout the Green zone, the distance covered increases very gradually, usually by only a quarter of a mile per workout. Distances range between half a mile and 1 mile, and your perceived exertion remains low, 1 to 3 on the RPE scale (55-69% of your max HR).

I'll introduce you to two types of walks in this section:

- **Easy.** This is a strolling pace—one that will ease you into walking. Allow yourself to meander slowly, without pressure to achieve a particular distance or check your watch. Be flexible. Stop to take a breather if you need to. Be gentle on yourself, allowing your body to get used to the simple walking motion. Think "easy does it" on the easy walks.

- **Steady.** The name says what it means. These are still easy walks, but they're done without breaks and at a continuous pace. Find the speed you can maintain within the range and stride off the distance. The only challenge is holding a steady pace. Speed is not a concern, although if you can't maintain 25-minute miles (2 mph), you should consider dropping back to easy walks to let your body and system build up to a steady pace.

The pace in Green workouts is a strolling 25- to 30-minute mile (2-2.4 mph). You will not be expending many calories, but you will be priming your body for longer and more intense workouts (if you want) that will use more energy. Either way, you will begin to gain health benefits from your first step forward. Remember that all calorie estimates are just that—estimates. Especially in Easy workouts, where breaks can't be calculated, the calories used will fluctuate.

Green Zone Preview				
Workout	**Description**	**Duration (minutes)**	**Distance (miles)**	**Intensity (% max HR/RPE)**
1	Easy walk	14-18	1/2	55-60/1
2	Easy walk	13-17	1/2	55-60/1
3	Easy walk	21-24	3/4	55-65/1-2
4	Easy walk	20-23	3/4	55-65/1-2
5	Easy walk	26-31	1	60-65/2
6	Steady walk	12-15	1/2	55-65/1-2
7	Steady walk	19-23	3/4	55-65/1-2
8	Steady walk	18-22	3/4	55-65/1-2
9	Steady walk	25-30	1	65-69/3
10	Treadmill/ Steady walk	25-26	1	65-69/3

WORKOUT 1

EASY WALK
TOTAL TIME: 25-30 minutes

1

WARM-UP: Roll your shoulders and march in place for 3 to 5 minutes, then stretch if desired.

WORKOUT
Distance: 1/2 mile
Walking time: 14-18 minutes
Pace: 25- to 30-minute miles
Effort: 55-60% max HR; RPE 1

COOL-DOWN: March in place, again rolling your shoulders, for 3 to 5 minutes, then stretch.

CALORIES USED: 35

COMMENTS
This is the first step in a walking program, intended only for beginners or those who haven't exercised in years. Feel free to take short breaks during your walk, or just slow down and literally smell the flowers. Use this walk to get used to being on your feet.

WORKOUT 2

2

EASY WALK
TOTAL TIME: 25-30 minutes

WARM-UP: Roll your shoulders and march in place for 3 to 5 minutes, then stretch if desired.

WORKOUT

Distance: 1/2 mile
Walking time: 13-17 minutes
Pace: 25- to 30-minute miles
Effort: 55-60% max HR; RPE 1

COOL-DOWN: March in place, again rolling your shoulders and shaking out your hands and arms, for 3 to 5 minutes, then stretch.

CALORIES USED: 35

COMMENTS

Although this walk is the same distance as Workout 1, try to take fewer breaks and complete it in a shorter time. Still, take short breaks as needed and breathe comfortably, maintaining only a light exertion.

WORKOUT 3

EASY WALK
TOTAL TIME: 30-35 minutes

3

WARM-UP: Roll your shoulders and march in place, or walk around your yard easily for 3 to 5 minutes, then stretch if desired.

WORKOUT
Distance: 3/4 mile
Walking time: 21-24 minutes
Pace: 25- to 30-minute miles
Effort: 55-65% max HR; RPE 1-2

COOL-DOWN: March in place, again rolling your shoulders and shaking out your hands and arms, for 3 to 5 minutes, then stretch.

CALORIES USED: 53

COMMENTS
Make sure you can complete the half-mile Workout 2 before increasing your distance. This workout is a quarter-mile longer; take plenty of short breaks to keep exertion light.

WORKOUT 4

EASY WALK
TOTAL TIME: 30-35 minutes

WARM-UP: Roll your shoulders and march in place, or walk around an open space easily for 3 to 5 minutes, then stretch if desired.

WORKOUT

Distance: 3/4 mile

Walking time: 20-23 minutes

Pace: 25- to 30-minute miles

Effort: 55-65% max HR; RPE 1-2

COOL-DOWN: March in place, again rolling your shoulders and shaking out your hands and arms, for 3 to 5 minutes, then stretch.

CALORIES USED: 53

COMMENTS

The time allotted for this workout allows only a couple of short rest stops, so you'll need to maintain a steadier clip throughout. Be very comfortable with this one before tackling Workout 5.

WORKOUT 5

EASY WALK
TOTAL TIME: 35-40 minutes

WARM-UP: Roll your shoulders and march in place, or walk around an open space easily for 3 to 5 minutes, then stretch if desired.

WORKOUT

Distance: 1 mile
Walking time: 26-31 minutes
Pace: 25- to 30-minute miles
Effort: 60-65% max HR; RPE 2

COOL-DOWN: March in place or circle your yard, living room, or any open space, for 3 to 5 minutes, again rolling your shoulders and shaking out your arms and hands before stopping to stretch.

CALORIES USED: 70

COMMENTS

This mile should be done with only a couple of short breaks. You should be able to complete it without a struggle.

WORKOUT 6

STEADY WALK
TOTAL TIME: 25-35 minutes

WARM-UP: Walk very easily around an open space for 4 to 5 minutes, then stretch if desired.

WORKOUT
Distance: 1/2 mile
Walking time: 12-15 minutes
Pace: 25- to 30-minute miles
Effort: 55-65% max HR; RPE 1-2

COOL-DOWN: Circle any open space for 4 to 5 minutes, shaking out your shoulders and hands before stopping to stretch.

CALORIES USED: 37

COMMENTS
This workout makes the transition to Steady walks. The distance drops again, but you should be able to finish this one without breaks and without feeling tired or winded.

WORKOUT 7

STEADY WALK
TOTAL TIME: 30-35 minutes

WARM-UP: Walk very easily back and forth or for a short distance for 4 to 5 minutes, then stretch if desired.

WORKOUT

Distance: 3/4 mile

Walking time: 19-23 minutes

Pace: 25- to 30-minute miles

Effort: 55-65% max HR; RPE 1-2

COOL-DOWN: Circle an open space for 4 to 5 minutes, shaking out your shoulders and hands before stopping to stretch.

CALORIES USED: 56

COMMENTS

Make sure your half-mile Steady walk in Workout 6 is successful before increasing the distance. Remember that the goal here is to maintain a steady, light-intensity walk without breaks.

WORKOUT 8

STEADY WALK
TOTAL TIME: 30-35 minutes

WARM-UP: Walk very easily back and forth or around an open space for 4 to 5 minutes, then stretch if desired.

WORKOUT

Distance: 3/4 mile

Walking time: 18-22 minutes

Pace: 25- to 30-minute miles

Effort: 55-65% max HR; RPE 1-2

COOL-DOWN: Circle an open space or walk another short distance for 4 to 5 minutes, shaking out your shoulders and hands before stopping to stretch.

CALORIES USED: 56

COMMENTS

Assuming your Steady walk of three quarters of a mile (Workout 7) was completed without difficulty, you're ready to move along. Keep the distance the same, but step up your pace slightly. As you go, remind yourself to relax your shoulders by giving them a shake now and then. Your exertion should remain light.

WORKOUT 9

STEADY WALK
TOTAL TIME: 35-45 minutes

9

WARM-UP: Walk very easily around an open area at the start of your route for 4 to 5 minutes, then stretch if desired.

WORKOUT

Distance: 1 mile
Walking time: 25-30 minutes
Pace: 25- to 30-minute miles
Effort: 65-69% max HR; RPE 3

COOL-DOWN: Stroll lightly, lifting and lowering your shoulders to relieve tension, for 4 to 5 minutes, then stretch.

CALORIES USED: 75

COMMENTS

Shoot for the low end in walking time, still keeping your perceived exertion light. You can repeat this workout several times, gradually lowering the speed from 30 to 25 minutes. Once you can complete the mile in 24 to 25 minutes, you're ready to tackle Blue workouts.

WORKOUT 10

10

TREADMILL/STEADY WALK
TOTAL TIME: 35-45 minutes

WARM-UP: Warm up by walking easily at about 1.8 mph (35-minute miles) for 4 to 5 minutes, then stretch if desired.

WORKOUT

Distance: 1 mile
Walking time: 25-26 minutes
Pace: 25- to 26-minute miles (2.3-2.4 mph)
Effort: 65-69% max HR; RPE 3

COOL-DOWN: Slow down the treadmill to 1.8 mph again, walking 4 to 5 minutes lightly while rolling your shoulders, then stretch.

CALORIES BURNED: 76

COMMENTS

Vary this workout as needed. Try to complete it at 2.4 mph, but lower the mph slightly (to 2.3 or 2.2) if your heart rate and perceived exertion start to climb.

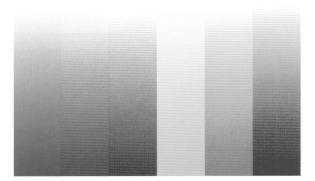

7

Blue Zone

Although Blue zone workouts increase in distance, the concept remains the same: low intensity with a low perceived exertion. The Blue workouts will have you picking up your pace slightly, so some of the shorter workouts aren't much longer in duration than Greens. Most, however, range from 30 to 35 minutes.

Still, the workouts are intended to be easily accomplished, and as such they're geared to the same walkers—beginners and those rehabilitating from injury or coming back to exercise after some time off. They also make good, easy workouts for intermediate or advanced walkers to use between hard days or as a quick pick-me-up.

The Blue workouts shouldn't be overly strenuous. If they are, try some additional Green workouts before moving on. Blue workouts cover distances of 1-1/4 to 2 miles, again increasing gradually, usually by only a quarter of a mile each workout. Your perceived exertion remains low, between about 1 and 3, with your maximum heart rate not exceeding 69%.

Like the Green workouts, most of the Blues are Easy and Steady walks. However, here I introduce you to one more type of walk, one that will resurface in the Yellow workouts:

- **Long.** A long workout should be slightly longer in both time and distance than your normal workouts. The definition of long, of course, will vary depending on your current average mileage. Here, 2-mile workouts are long. Later, 4 miles is long, and in the advanced Red workouts, 13 miles becomes the long challenge.

You should be able to complete a Long workout at a steady pace, without rest stops. The pace should be comfortable, allowing you to talk to a friend or just enjoy the passing scenery. Whatever your level, a Long walk should never exceed about a third of your weekly mileage. So if you are covering about 6 miles in a week, the Blue Long walks of 2 miles are perfect.

Blue Zone Preview				
Workout	Description	Duration (minutes)	Distance (miles)	Intensity (% max HR/RPE)
1	Easy walk	26-29	1-1/4	60-65/2
2	Easy walk	31-34	1-1/2	60-65/2
3	Easy walk	36-37	1-3/4	60-69/2-3
4	Steady walk	25-26	1-1/4	60-69/2-3
5	Steady walk	30-31	1-1/2	60-69/2-3
6	Steady walk	27-30	1-1/2	60-69/2-3
7	Steady walk	32-35	1-3/4	60-69/2-3
8	Long walk	38	2	65-69/3
9	Long walk	38	2	65-69/3
10	Treadmill/ Steady walk	28	1-1/2	60-69/2-3

WORKOUT 1

EASY WALK
TOTAL TIME: 35-45 minutes

WARM-UP: Walk very easily about 4 to 5 minutes, then stretch if desired.

WORKOUT

Distance: 1-1/4 miles
Walking time: 26-29 minutes
Pace: 20- to 22-minute miles
Effort: 60-65% max HR; RPE 2

COOL-DOWN: Walk easily for 4 to 5 minutes, shaking out your arms, then stretch.

CALORIES USED: 100

COMMENTS

Notice that the pace picks up slightly as the distance increases. Still, allow yourself to get used to both by taking several breaks as needed.

WORKOUT 2

2

EASY WALK
TOTAL TIME: 45-50 minutes

WARM-UP: Walk very easily about 4 to 5 minutes, then stretch if desired.

WORKOUT

Distance: 1-1/2 miles
Walking time: 31-34 minutes
Pace: 20- to 22-minute miles
Effort: 60-65% max HR; RPE 2

COOL-DOWN: Walk easily for 4 to 5 minutes, dropping your chin forward and your head from side to side to relax your neck, then stretch.

CALORIES USED: 120

COMMENTS

This workout challenges you to stay closer to the 21-minute mile and take fewer breaks, perhaps only two of 30 seconds each. Listen to your body, though, and go slower if it demands it.

WORKOUT 3

EASY WALK
TOTAL TIME: 50 minutes

3

WARM-UP: Walk very easily about 4 to 5 minutes, then stretch if desired.

WORKOUT

Distance: 1-3/4 miles
Walking time: 36-37 minutes
Pace: 20-minute miles
Effort: 60-69% max HR; RPE 2-3

COOL-DOWN: Walk easily for 4 to 5 minutes, dropping your chin forward and your head from side to side to relax your neck, then stretch.

CALORIES USED: 140

COMMENTS

Try to step a bit faster, this time edging closer to the 20-minute mile, while still allowing yourself several rest stops. The goal is to complete the distance.

STEADY WALK
TOTAL TIME: 35-45 minutes

WARM-UP: Walk very easily for about 5 minutes, then stretch if desired.

WORKOUT

Distance: 1-1/4 miles
Walking time: 25-26 minutes
Pace: 20- to 21-minute miles
Effort: 60-69% max HR; RPE 2-3

COOL-DOWN: Walk easily for 4 to 5 minutes, letting the front of your foot flap onto the ground to relax your shins, then stretch.

CALORIES USED: 100

COMMENTS

As you pick up your pace and eliminate breaks during the walk, you might need more warm-up. Don't shortchange the easy warm-up walk and loosening stretches. They can make or break your workout!

WORKOUT 5

STEADY WALK

TOTAL TIME: 35-45 minutes

5

WARM-UP: Walk very easily for about 5 minutes, then stretch if desired.

WORKOUT

Distance: 1-1/2 miles

Walking time: 30-31 minutes

Pace: 20- to 21-minute miles

Effort: 60-69% max HR; RPE 2-3

COOL-DOWN: Walk easily for 4 to 5 minutes, letting the front of your foot flap onto the ground to relax your shins, then stretch.

CALORIES USED: 120

COMMENTS

Maintain the slightly faster pace for another quarter of a mile. If this is too much, try Blue Workout 2 a few times again.

WORKOUT 6

6

STEADY WALK
TOTAL TIME: 40-45 minutes

WARM-UP: Walk very easily for about 5 to 7 minutes, then stretch if desired.

WORKOUT

Distance: 1-1/2 miles

Walking time: 27-30 minutes

Pace: 18- to 20-minute miles

Effort: 60-69% max HR; RPE 2-3

COOL-DOWN: Walk easily for 5 minutes, rolling your shoulders back to stretch the front of your chest, then stretch.

CALORIES USED: 125

COMMENTS

Same distance as Workout 5, but pick up the pace again to edge your RPE toward 3. Try concentrating on the speed of your arm swing to get your feet to move.

WORKOUT 7

STEADY WALK
TOTAL TIME: 45-55 minutes

7

WARM-UP: Walk very easily for about 5 to 7 minutes, then stretch if desired.

WORKOUT

Distance: 1-3/4 miles
Walking time: 32-35 minutes
Pace: 18- to 20-minute miles
Effort: 60-69% max HR; RPE 2-3

COOL-DOWN: Walk easily for 5 minutes, rolling your shoulders backward to stretch the front of your chest, then stretch.

CALORIES USED: 145

COMMENTS

The pace keeps you moving. Make sure you can complete this comfortably before trying a longer walk.

WORKOUT 8

8

LONG WALK
TOTAL TIME: 50-55 minutes

WARM-UP: Walk very easily about 5 to 7 minutes, then stretch if desired.

WORKOUT

Distance: 2 miles

Walking time: 38 minutes

Pace: 18- to 20-minute miles (see comments)

Effort: 65-69% max HR; RPE 3

Terrain: A short, gradual hill in the second mile, if available

COOL-DOWN: Walk easily for 5 to 7 minutes, then stretch.

CALORIES USED: 160 (180 with a slight incline)

COMMENTS

Maintain the faster 18-minute-mile pace for the first mile, if possible, then allow yourself to finish the second mile at a 20-minute pace. Your cool-down will be extra important after this one; make sure you also take the time to stretch.

WORKOUT 9

LONG WALK
TOTAL TIME: 50-55 minutes

9

WARM-UP: Walk very easily about 5 to 7 minutes, then stretch if desired.

WORKOUT

Distance: 2 miles

Walking time: 38 minutes

Pace: 18- to 20-minute miles (see comments)

Effort: 65-69% max HR; RPE 3

Terrain: A short, gradual hill in the first mile, if available

COOL-DOWN: Walk easily for 5 to 7 minutes, then stretch.

CALORIES USED: 160 (180 with a slight incline)

COMMENTS

In this walk, start out at a slower 20-minute-mile pace for the first mile, then pick it up to the faster 18-minute-mile pace in the second. This is tougher than slowing down at the end, so be sure you can do Blue Workout 7 before trying this challenge.

10 TREADMILL/STEADY WALK
TOTAL TIME: 35-40 minutes

WARM-UP: Walk very easily (2 mph) for about 5 minutes, then stretch if desired.

WORKOUT

Distance: 1-1/2 miles
Walking time: 28 minutes
Pace: 18- to 20-minute miles (3-3.4 mph; see comments)
Effort: 60-69% max HR; RPE 2-3
Resistance: A 3-4% grade in the last half-mile

COOL-DOWN: Walk easily (2 mph) for 5 minutes, then stretch.

CALORIES USED: 150

COMMENTS

Consider this a middle-of-the-road Blue workout. Challenge yourself to finish the first mile in 18 minutes (3.3-3.4 mph), then drop to a 20-minute-mile pace (3 mph) for the last half-mile. If your heart rate is not too high, set the treadmill for a 3-4% grade during the last half-mile.

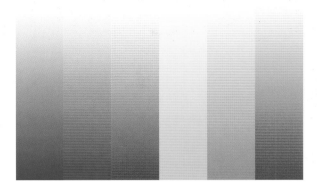

Purple Zone

With Purple workouts, you'll be stepping up a notch in intensity. Your perceived exertion will climb several rungs to a range of 4 to 5 or about 70 to 79% of your maximum heart rate. You should still feel as if you can converse, but you may need to stop between phrases or sentences for occasional breath breaks. You certainly shouldn't feel as if you can sing!

These workouts are the middle ground between the light intensity of the Green and Blue zones and the high intensity of Orange and Red. Along with a few longer Yellow zone workouts, they might be all you'll need for your exercise regimen. They cover up to 2-1/4 miles and last less than 35 minutes, with most walks lasting about 25 to 30 minutes.

As was true of the Green zone workouts, these will fit easily into lunch hours and coffee breaks or between meetings. They will let you get your health break without taking lots of time from family and work.

Easy walks, those that allow a meandering pace with rest stops, are not part of the Purple zone. We will continue with Steady walks and add two more types:

- **Tempo.** A Tempo walk is much like a Steady one in that you determine the pace you can maintain for the distance and hold it. But with a Tempo walk you'll pick a brisk pace, one that's just a bit higher than the totally comfortable one you'd select for a Steady walk. Although not fast, these should be nonstop, and you should feel your breathing and heart rate increase. But you still should be able to converse without being breathless.

• **Speed Play.** Speed play is what its name implies: You get to tinker with speedier bursts of walking. Similar to the disciplined interval workouts of runners on tracks, speed play is a less structured style that uses the natural terrain and environment. These walks should challenge your technique and speed yet remain fun and playful.

Because the bursts of speed are short, your perceived exertion should still average no higher than 5, although you may feel yourself drifting a little higher during your playful speed. Remember, speed here is relative. This is not a race, just a way for you to experiment with your potential and see how it feels.

For the more advanced walker, Speed Play walks can be short, efficient sessions to maintain fitness when the time is not available for more intense or longer workouts. Advanced walkers might make their speedy bursts quite fast for more of a challenge.

Because you'll be varying your pace during some of the walks in the Purple zone, you will spend some of your walking time "recovering." Recovery happens between speedy bursts; it should be slow enough to allow your body to return to steady state. That means your breathing and heart rate will slow slightly, allowing you to again pick up your speed to your Steady walk pace.

Purple Zone Preview				
Workout	Description	Duration (minutes)	Distance (miles)	Intensity (% max HR/RPE)
1	Steady walk	25-27	1-1/2	70-74/4
2	Steady walk	27-30	1-3/4	70-74/4
3	Steady walk	32-36	2	70-74/4
4	Tempo walk	23-24	1-1/2	70-79/4-5
5	Tempo walk	30-31	2	70-79/4-5
6	Tempo walk	34	2-1/4	75-79/5
7	Speed Play walk	24-26	1-1/2	75-79/5 (average)
8	Speed Play walk	23-25	1-1/2	75-79/5 (average)
9	Speed Play walk	30-32	2	75-79/5 (average)
10	Treadmill/Speed Play–Tempo walk	30-32	2	75-79/5 (average)

WORKOUT 1

STEADY WALK
TOTAL TIME: 35-40 minutes

1

WARM-UP: Walk for about 4 to 5 minutes at a pace slightly slower than your Steady walk pace, then stretch if desired.

WORKOUT
Distance: 1-1/2 miles
Walking time: 25-27 minutes
Pace: 15- to 18-minute miles
Effort: 70-74% max HR; RPE 4

COOL-DOWN: Walk easily for 5 minutes, then stretch.

CALORIES USED: 130

COMMENTS
The workouts in this zone are slightly faster, so use this one and the next to feel that pace. Start with an 18- or even 19-minute-mile pace, speed up to 16-minute miles, then slow back down to 18-minute miles. The pace should be relatively smooth, without noticeable bursts.

WORKOUT 2

2

STEADY WALK
TOTAL TIME: 40 minutes

WARM-UP: Walk for about 4 to 5 minutes at a pace slightly slower than your Steady walk, then stretch if desired.

WORKOUT
Distance: 1-3/4 miles
Walking time: 27-30 minutes
Pace: 15- to 18-minute miles
Effort: 70-74% max HR; RPE 4

COOL-DOWN: Walk easily for 5 minutes, then stretch.

CALORIES USED: 150

COMMENTS
As in Workout 1, you will experiment with finding the faster pace without pressure to perform it the entire time. Remember to think "faster feet," not longer strides.

WORKOUT 3

STEADY WALK
TOTAL TIME: 40-50 minutes

3

WARM-UP: Walk for about 4 to 5 minutes at a pace slightly slower than your Steady walk, then stretch if desired.

WORKOUT

Distances: 2 miles
Walking time: 32-36 minutes
Pace: 16- to 17-minute miles
Effort: 70-74% max HR; RPE 4

COOL-DOWN: Walk easily for 5 minutes, then stretch.

CALORIES USED: 165

COMMENTS

In duration, this is the longest workout in the Purple zone. Experiment with some hill resistance in the middle section if there is a hill handy. With hill or without, try to keep this walk closer to 16- or 17-minute miles as a transition to the upcoming Tempo walks.

TEMPO WALK
TOTAL TIME: 35 minutes

WARM-UP: Walk for about 5 to 7 minutes at a pace slightly slower than your Steady walk, then stretch if desired.

WORKOUT

Distance: 1-1/2 miles
Walking time: 23-24 minutes
Pace: 15- to 16-minute miles
Effort: 70-79% max HR; RPE 4-5

COOL-DOWN: Walk easily for 5 to 7 minutes, then stretch.

CALORIES USED: 130

COMMENTS

As you tackle this first Tempo walk, think fast feet and powerful arms to keep you going at 15-minute miles. If you can't hold a faster pace while maintaining an RPE no higher than 5, try a few more of the slower paced Steady walks.

WORKOUT 5

TEMPO WALK
TOTAL TIME: 40 minutes

5

WARM-UP: Walk for about 5 to 7 minutes at a pace slightly slower than your Steady walk, then stretch if desired.

WORKOUT

Distance: 2 miles
Walking time: 30-31 minutes
Pace: 15- to 16-minute miles
Effort: 70-79% max HR; RPE 4-5
Terrain: A short, gradual incline in the last mile

COOL-DOWN: Walk easily for 5 to 7 minutes, then stretch.

CALORIES USED: 170 (210 with gradual incline)

COMMENTS

Make sure you keep your shoulders relaxed as you tackle this one at a 15-minute-mile pace. Expect to slow down slightly on the incline—perhaps to 16-minute miles—but don't stroll into it. Practice your rear toe pushoff as you stride uphill.

TEMPO WALK
TOTAL TIME: 45 minutes

WARM-UP: Walk for about 5 to 7 minutes at a pace slightly slower than your Steady walk, then stretch if desired.

WORKOUT

Distance: 2-1/4 miles
Walking time: 34 minutes
Pace: 15-minute miles
Effort: 75-79% max HR; RPE 5

COOL-DOWN: Walk easily for 5 to 7 minutes, then stretch.

CALORIES USED: 195

COMMENTS

You should be able to maintain 15-minute miles for this workout. If not, tackle the shorter Workout 4 and build confidence that you can maintain the pace.

WORKOUT 7

SPEED PLAY WALK
TOTAL TIME: 35-40 minutes

7

WARM-UP: Walk for about 5 minutes at a pace slightly slower than your Steady walk, another minute at your Steady pace, then stretch.

WORKOUT

Distance: 1-1/2 miles

Walking time: 24-26 minutes

Pace: 17- to 18-minute miles, with 15-second medium-hard bursts of 15-minute miles every 5 minutes

Effort: 75-79% max HR; RPE 5 (average)

COOL-DOWN: Walk easily for 5 to 7 minutes, then stretch.

CALORIES USED: 135

COMMENTS

Notice that the end of your warm-up is done a little quicker to prepare your body for Speed Play. Try only very short bursts this first time, and allow yourself to recover with a slower but Steady pace between the bursts.

WORKOUT 8

8

SPEED PLAY WALK
TOTAL TIME: 35-40 minutes

WARM-UP: Walk for about 5 minutes at a pace slightly slower than your Steady walk, another minute at your Steady pace, then stretch.

WORKOUT

Distance: 1-1/2 miles

Walking time: 23-25 minutes

Pace: 17- to 18-minute miles, with 30-second medium-hard bursts of 15-minute miles every 4 to 5 minutes

Effort: 75-79% max HR; RPE 5 (average)

COOL-DOWN: Walk easily for 5 to 7 minutes, then stretch.

CALORIES USED: 135

COMMENTS

Lengthen the speedier bursts, but keep the intervals between them Steady. Think about strong feet grabbing the ground and pulling it behind you during the Speed Play.

WORKOUT 9

SPEED PLAY WALK
TOTAL TIME: 40-45 minutes

9

WARM-UP: Walk for about 5 minutes at a pace slightly slower than your Steady walk, another minute at your Steady pace, then stretch.

WORKOUT

Distance: 2 miles

Walking time: 30-32 minutes

Pace: 17-minute miles, with 1-minute bursts of 15-minute miles every 4 to 5 minutes. (The bursts should be medium-hard but not all-out.)

Effort: 75-79% max HR; RPE 5 (average)

COOL-DOWN: Walk easily for 5 to 7 minutes, then stretch.

CALORIES USED: 170

COMMENTS

Make sure you're comfortable with 30-second Speed Play before graduating to 1-minute bursts. Your goal is to keep the walk between bursts slightly more up-tempo.

10

TREADMILL/SPEED PLAY—
TEMPO WALK
TOTAL TIME: 40-45 minutes

WARM-UP: Walk for about 5 minutes at about 3.0-3.2 mph, another minute at about 3.4, then stretch.

WORKOUT

Distance: 2 miles

Walking time: 30-32 minutes

Pace: Alternating 16- and 17-minute miles (3.7 and 3.5 mph) with 30-second bursts of 15-minute miles (4 mph) every 5 minutes

Effort: 75-79% max HR; RPE 5 (average)

Resistance: 2-3% grade in one recovery interval (see comments)

COOL-DOWN: Walk easily for 5 to 7 minutes, then stretch.

CALORIES USED: 170

COMMENTS

You can easily clock your speed using the treadmill. Start with 5 minutes at 3.5 mph, then do a speedy interval, then another 5 minutes at 3.7 mph. Alternate this pattern, doing six Speed Plays. Try a hill in one 3.5-mph interval.

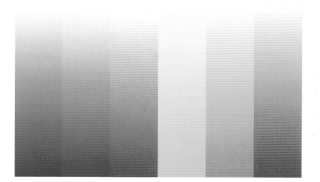

Yellow Zone

Yellow zone workouts are intended for the more intermediate walker, perhaps one who is looking for a few additional challenges such as speed bursts or longer duration. The following workouts will also fit well into the schedule for an advanced walker looking for a lighter, active-recovery day (an easy workout between harder ones). A beginner who wants to try a weekend challenge could tackle one of the first few workouts, keeping in mind the need to modify the speed or take breaks. If you were able to accomplish the previous Purple workouts, you should be able to successfully complete Yellow ones.

The intensity of the workouts in the Yellow zone is about the same as the Purple zone workouts. The RPE range is 4 to 5, or about 70 to 79% of your maximum heart rate. But in this zone, you'll be completing longer walks. Yellow zone walks are a good transition if your goal is to someday accomplish workouts in the Orange or Red zones.

As longer duration walks, the Yellow workouts cover up to 4-1/4 miles and last between 35 and 62 minutes. Try one of these in the morning before you start your day, at the end of the day before dinner, or for an extra lengthy walk on a weekend.

Yellow zone walks are much like those in the Purple zone, just longer. You'll continue with Steady walks. You're familiar with the continuous but comfortable pace these require (as introduced in the three previous chapters). Tempo walks, too, remain part of the Yellow zone. A Speed Play walk is tossed in only for a little variety before you move on to Long walks, the real meat of the workouts. If you recall from the introduction to the Blue zone, Long walks are slightly longer in time and distance than your normal walk, but they should not exceed about a third of your weekly mileage. As usual, I've also offered one workout on a treadmill.

Your "goal pace," as you'll see come up in the Yellow workouts, means the speed that is your goal for that workout.

Yellow Zone Preview				
Workout	Description	Duration (minutes)	Distance (miles)	Intensity (% max HR/RPE)
1	Steady walk	37-38	2-1/2	70-74/4
2	Steady walk	44-45	3	70-74/4
3	Tempo walk	35-36	2-1/2	70-79/4-5
4	Tempo walk	42-43	3	70-79/4-5
5	Speed Play walk	41-42	3	75-79/5 (average)
6	Long walk	52-53	3-1/2	75-79/5
7	Long walk	56-57	3-3/4	75-79/5
8	Long walk	56-57	4	75-79/5
9	Long walk	60-62	4-1/4	75-79/5
10	Treadmill/ Long walk	52-55	3-1/2	70-79/4-5

STEADY WALK

TOTAL TIME: 50-55 minutes

1

WARM-UP: Walk for about 5 to 7 minutes at a pace slower than your goal pace for this walk, or make the first half-mile of the workout slower. Stretch if desired.

WORKOUT

Distance: 2-1/2 miles
Walking time: 37-38 minutes
Pace: 14- to 15-minute miles
Effort: 70-74% max HR; RPE 4

COOL-DOWN: Walk easily for 5 to 7 minutes, then stretch.

CALORIES USED: 230

COMMENTS

This is a good transition into Yellow workouts—a moderate pace for beginning walkers to see how far they've come or for advanced walkers to take a break. Forget hills; just keep the pace steady and more brisk than in the past.

2

STEADY WALK

TOTAL TIME: 55-65 minutes

WARM-UP: Walk for about 5 to 7 minutes at a pace slower than your goal pace for the day, or make the first half-mile of the workout slower. Stretch if desired.

WORKOUT

Distance: 3 miles
Walking time: 44-45 minutes
Pace: 14- to 15-minute miles
Effort: 70-74% max HR; RPE 4

COOL-DOWN: Walk easily for 5 to 7 minutes, then stretch.

CALORIES USED: 275

COMMENTS

Stretch out this walk, aiming for the 2 miles to be closer to a 14-1/2-minute pace; then allow yourself to drop to a 15-minute pace in the last mile.

WORKOUT 3

TEMPO WALK
TOTAL TIME: 50-60 minutes

3

WARM-UP: Walk for about 5 to 7 minutes at a pace slower than your goal pace for the day, or make the first half-mile of the workout slower. Stretch if desired.

WORKOUT

Distance: 2-1/2 miles
Walking time: 35-36 minutes
Pace: 14- to 15-minute miles
Effort: 70-79% max HR; RPE 4-5

COOL-DOWN: Walk easily for 5 to 7 minutes, then stretch.

CALORIES USED: 235

COMMENTS

Return to thinking about moving your feet faster to keep the pace. Your goal is to stick closer to 14-minute miles, although slowing the pace slightly in the last half-mile will help you finish.

WORKOUT 4

TEMPO WALK
TOTAL TIME: 55-65 minutes

WARM-UP: Walk for about 5 to 7 minutes at a pace slower than your goal pace for the day, or make the first half-mile of the workout slower. Stretch if desired.

WORKOUT

Distance: 3 miles

Walking time: 42-43 minutes

Pace: 14- to 15-minute miles

Effort: 70-79% max HR; RPE 4-5

Terrain: Gradual inclines, if available

COOL-DOWN: Walk easily for 5 to 7 minutes, then stretch.

CALORIES USED: 280 (350 with some gradual hills)

COMMENTS

Aim for the 14-minute pace again, but if you find some minor inclines to incorporate, your pace will slow slightly. Lean into the hill, but not from your waist, and use the incline to concentrate on a powerful back toe pushoff.

WORKOUT 5

SPEED PLAY WALK
TOTAL TIME: 55-60 minutes

5

WARM-UP: Walk for about 5 to 7 minutes at a pace slower than your 15-minute-mile pace, picking up the pace slightly toward the end, then stretch.

WORKOUT

Distance: 3 miles

Walking time: 41-42 minutes

Pace: 15-minute miles, with 1-minute bursts of 14-minute miles every 4 to 5 minutes.

Effort: 75-79% max HR; RPE 5 (average)

COOL-DOWN: Walk easily for 5 to 7 minutes, then stretch.

CALORIES USED: 285

COMMENTS

Use this walk at any time to help you practice 14-minute miles. This conditions your system for holding the speed in the longer walks to come.

WORKOUT 6

LONG WALK
TOTAL TIME: 65-70 minutes

WARM-UP: Walk for about 5 to 7 minutes at a pace slower than your goal pace, relaxing your shoulders and visualizing your success at this first longer walk. Stretch if desired.

WORKOUT
Distance: 3-1/2 miles
Walking time: 52-53 minutes
Pace: 15-minute miles
Effort: 75-79% max HR; RPE 5

COOL-DOWN: Walk easily for 5 to 7 minutes, then stretch.

CALORIES USED: 315

COMMENTS
Don't push yourself to go too fast, especially in the beginning when you feel fresh. The goal is to finish still feeling energized.

WORKOUT 7

LONG WALK
TOTAL TIME: 70-75 minutes

WARM-UP: Walk for about 5 to 7 minutes at a pace slower than your goal pace, relaxing your shoulders. Stretch if desired.

WORKOUT

Distance: 3-3/4 miles
Walking time: 56-57 minutes
Pace: 14- to 15-minute miles
Effort: 75-79% max HR; RPE 5

COOL-DOWN: Walk easily for 5 to 7 minutes, then stretch.

CALORIES USED: 340

COMMENTS

Don't increase the distance or speed of your Long walk until you're comfortable with Yellow Workout 6. With this one, try to start with a faster pace, then let yourself slow in the last half. Remember, the back toe pushoff remains strong now, even on flat terrain.

8

LONG WALK
TOTAL TIME: 70-75 minutes

WARM-UP: Walk for about 5 to 7 minutes at a pace slower than your goal pace, sensing the rolling motion in your feet. Stretch if desired.

WORKOUT

Distance: 4 miles
Walking time: 56-57 minutes
Pace: 14- to 15-minute miles
Effort: 75-79% max HR; RPE 5

COOL-DOWN: Walk easily for 5 to 7 minutes, then stretch.

CALORIES USED: 360

COMMENTS

Tackle this one with the intention to complete the entire distance at a steady clip. With walks heading toward an hour now, you might want to find a friend to take along.

WORKOUT 9

LONG WALK
TOTAL TIME: 75-80 minutes

WARM-UP: Walk for about 5 to 7 minutes at a pace slower than your goal pace, sensing the rolling motion in your feet from heel to toe. Stretch if desired.

WORKOUT

Distance: 4-1/4 miles
Walking time: 60-62 minutes
Pace: 14-minute miles
Effort: 75-79% max HR; RPE 5

COOL-DOWN: Walk easily for 5 to 7 minutes, then stretch.

CALORIES USED: 390

COMMENTS

This is one of the last of this section's Long walks; you should be able to maintain nearly a 14-minute pace, still keeping this workout to an hour.

WORKOUT 10

10 TREADMILL/LONG WALK
TOTAL TIME: 65-70 minutes

WARM-UP: Walk for about 5 minutes at a pace slower than your goal pace (3.3-3.5 mph), then stretch if desired.

WORKOUT

Distance: 3-1/2 miles

Walking time: 52-55 minutes

Pace: 14- to 15-minute miles (4-4.3 mph). Slow your pace to 3.8-4 mph on the inclines.

Effort: 70-79% max HR; RPE 4-5

Resistance: 3-4% incline for 3-4 minutes every 10 minutes

COOL-DOWN: Walk easily for 5 minutes, then stretch.

CALORIES USED: 345

COMMENTS

Use the treadmill for a longer workout if the weather is bad or if you'd like to control the hills. If the treadmill is near a mirror, watch your arms and feet to assess your form.

10

Orange Zone

If you're going to tackle Orange workouts, you're an advanced walker. You probably walk for your primary form of exercise or are fit enough to undertake very challenging athletic walks a couple of times a week. It's likely you've been walking for fitness for many months or even years.

These Orange workouts are intended to give you an extra push in your daily routine. But they are not to be done every day, because they are too high in intensity. Still, because the walks are shorter (none longer than 45 minutes, with most around 30), they can fit in easily after a long day or even in a long lunch break. They cover up to 3-1/2 miles.

In the Orange zone you will work at very strong intensities, with workouts ranging in perceived exertion between 6 and 8 on the RPE scale, or 80% to 94% of your maximum heart rate. This means take extra care in listening to your body to avoid overexertion that could lead to injury or strain.

Many of the walks are the Speed Plays that were first introduced in the Purple zone. Here you'll make your speedy segments last longer. But don't forget the importance of recovery between speed intervals (remember that idea from the Purple zone?).

We'll also introduce another walk:

- **Challenge Tempo.** These walks are meant to be little races with yourself. Like the Tempo walks you've already done, these will challenge you to upgrade that already upbeat Tempo pace a few notches. Challenge Tempo walks are best done as part of weekend walk/run events put on in every community, where the energy of a crowd will push you along.

As elsewhere, I've included one version on a treadmill for those days when you want to, or have to, stay indoors. Warm-ups will also increase in intensity, although you'll still start at a very easy speed.

Orange Zone Preview				
Workout	Description	Duration (minutes)	Distance (miles)	Intensity (% max HR/RPE)
1	Speed Play walk	26-28	2	80-84/6 (average)
2	Speed Play walk	32-35	2-1/2	80-84/6 (average)
3	Speed Play walk	32-35	2-1/2	80-84/6 (average)
4	Speed Play walk	40-42	3	85-89/7 (average)
5	Speed Play– Tempo walk	39-40	3-1/2	85-89/7 (average)
6	Challenge Tempo walk	27	2	80-89/6-7
7	Challenge Tempo walk	26	2	80-89/6-7
8	Challenge Tempo walk	43-44	3.1	85-89/7
9	Challenge Tempo walk	40-42	3.1	85-89/7
10	Treadmill/Challenge Tempo walk	34	2-1/2	85-89/7

WORKOUT 1

SPEED PLAY WALK
TOTAL TIME: 40-45 minutes

1

WARM-UP: Walk for about 5 minutes at a slow pace, stretch, then walk another 2 minutes at a more moderate pace, picking it up even faster for your final 30 seconds.

WORKOUT

Distance: 2 miles

Walking time: 26-28 minutes

Pace: 13- to 14-minute miles. Time yourself at 2-minute bursts close to 13-minute miles, alternating with 6 minutes at the easier pace.

Effort: 80-84% max HR; RPE 6 (average)

COOL-DOWN: Walk easily for 5 to 7 minutes, then stretch.

CALORIES USED: 190

COMMENTS

Be sure to check your perceived exertion and heart rate. Both should be at the bottom end of their given ranges before your next burst. If not, take another minute or so to recover. If your perceived exertion and heart rate reach the lower end more quickly, try shortening the recovery period.

WORKOUT 2

2

SPEED PLAY WALK
TOTAL TIME: 45-50 minutes

WARM-UP: Walk for about 5 minutes at a slow pace, stretch, then walk for another 2 minutes at a more moderate pace, picking it up even faster for the last 30 seconds.

WORKOUT

Distance: 2-1/2 miles

Walking time: 32-35 minutes

Pace: 13- to 14-minute miles. Time yourself at 3-minute bursts close to 13-minute miles, alternating with 7 minutes at the easier pace.

Effort: 80-84% max HR; RPE 6 (average)

COOL-DOWN: Walk easily for 5 to 7 minutes, then stretch.

CALORIES USED: 240

COMMENTS

Remember fast-moving arms and feet to keep propelling you forward. Go back to Workout 1 if your heart rate doesn't drop about 10 beats per minute in recovery.

WORKOUT 3

SPEED PLAY WALK
TOTAL TIME: 45-50 minutes

3

WARM-UP: Walk for about 5 minutes at a slow pace, stretch, then walk for another 2 minutes at a more moderate pace, picking it up even faster for the last 30 seconds.

WORKOUT

Distance: 2-1/2 miles

Walking time: 32-35 minutes

Pace: 13- to 14-minute miles. Time yourself at 3-minute bursts close to 13-minute miles, alternating with 7 minutes at the easier pace.

Effort: 80-84% max HR; RPE 6 (average)

Terrain: Gradual inclines on several intervals

COOL-DOWN: Walk easily for 5 to 7 minutes, then stretch.

CALORIES USED: 265

COMMENTS

Same length and pace as Workout 2, but push yourself up small hills on the speedy bursts. Lean into the incline from your ankles and use your arm and back muscles for power, as well as the toe pushing behind you. If you walk in a two-story mall, use stairs to achieve the intensity bursts.

WORKOUT 4

SPEED PLAY WALK
TOTAL TIME: 55-60 minutes

WARM-UP: Walk for about 5 minutes at a slow pace, stretch, then walk for another 2 minutes at a more moderate pace, picking it up even faster for the last 30 seconds.

WORKOUT

Distance: 3 miles

Walking time: 40-42 minutes

Pace: 13- to 14-minute miles. Time yourself at 4-minute bursts no slower than 13-minute miles, alternating with 8 minutes at the easier, but still brisk, pace.

Effort: 85-89% max HR; RPE 7 (average)

COOL-DOWN: Walk easily for 5 to 7 minutes, then stretch.

CALORIES USED: 295

COMMENTS

Use the easy but brisk recovery to give you the strength to push hard during the Speed Play. Experiment with shorter recovery periods as you become more fit and your perceived exertion and heart rate drop more quickly.

WORKOUT 5

SPEED PLAY–TEMPO WALK
TOTAL TIME: 55-60 minutes

5

WARM-UP: Walk for about 5 minutes at a slow pace, stretch, then walk for another 2 minutes at a more moderate pace, picking it up even faster for the last 30 seconds.

WORKOUT

Distance: 3-1/2 miles
Walking time: 39-40 minutes
Pace: Close to 13-minute miles, with 40-second to 1-minute segments nearly as hard as you can. Allow 3 to 4 minutes of recovery after each burst.
Effort: 85-89% max HR; RPE 7 (average)

COOL-DOWN: Walk easily for 5 to 7 minutes, then stretch.

CALORIES USED: 350

COMMENTS

Don't pick such a hard pace for the 1-minute sprints that you can't keep a steady pace. These are fast but not quite all-out. During the 3- to 4-minute recovery breaks, try to keep the pace close to 13-minute miles. Your heart rate will drop only a few beats. This is for advanced-intermediate walkers nearly ready for Workouts 6-9.

CHALLENGE TEMPO WALK
TOTAL TIME: 40 minutes

WARM-UP: Walk for about 5 minutes at a slow pace, stretch, then walk for another 2 to 3 minutes at a more moderate pace, picking it up even faster for the last minute. Finish your warm-up right before the start.

WORKOUT

Distances: 2 miles

Walking time: 27 minutes

Pace: First mile, steady 14-minute mile; second mile, 13-minute mile

Effort: 80-89% max HR; RPE 6-7

COOL-DOWN: Walk easily for 5 to 7 minutes, then stretch.

CALORIES USED: 195

COMMENTS

Pick a weekend event with a 2-mile walk, or just do the first 2 miles of a 5-kilometer (3.1-mile) race. Take a few deep breaths to relax yourself as you stand at the starting line, otherwise you may start too fast from the excitement and tire too soon.

WORKOUT 7

CHALLENGE TEMPO WALK
TOTAL TIME: 40 minutes

7

WARM-UP: Walk for about 5 minutes at a slow pace, stretch, then walk for another 2 to 3 minutes at a more moderate pace, picking it up even faster for the last minute. Finish your warm-up right before the start.

WORKOUT

Distance: 2 miles
Walking time: 26 minutes
Pace: 13-minute miles
Effort: 80-89% max HR; RPE 6-7
Terrain: Rolling hills if possible

COOL-DOWN: Walk easily for 5 to 7 minutes, then stretch.

CALORIES USED: 200 (250 with rolling hills)

COMMENTS

Choose an event as you did in Workout 6. No easy start with a slower first mile this time, though. Still, don't let your adrenalin get the best of you so that you start too fast and burn yourself out. Try this on an event course with rolling hills for an extra challenge. As you advance, try to complete an entire 5K walk.

WORKOUT 8

8 CHALLENGE TEMPO WALK
TOTAL TIME: 55-60 minutes

WARM-UP: Walk for about 5 minutes at a slow pace, stretch, then walk for another 2 to 3 minutes at a more moderate pace, picking it up even faster for the last minute. Finish your warm-up right before the start.

WORKOUT

Distance: 5-kilometer (3.1-mile) event
Walking time: 43-44 minutes
Pace: 14-minute miles
Effort: 85-89% max HR; RPE 7
Terrain: Rolling hills

COOL-DOWN: Walk easily for 5 to 7 minutes, then stretch.

CALORIES USED: 285 (350 with rolling hills)

COMMENTS

Stick to about 14-minute miles, which will be a good pace on a route with rolling hills. If you feel good in the last half-mile, pick up your speed a little. (Bet you'll beat some joggers!) Don't neglect the cool-down, which is absolutely necessary after more intense workouts.

WORKOUT 9

CHALLENGE TEMPO WALK
TOTAL TIME: 55-60 minutes

9

WARM-UP: Walk for about 5 minutes at a slow pace, stretch, then walk for another 2 to 3 minutes at a more moderate pace, picking it up even faster for the last minute. Finish your warm-up right before the start.

WORKOUT

Distance: 5-kilometer (3.1-mile) event
Walking time: 40-42 minutes
Pace: 13-minute miles
Effort: 85-89% max HR; RPE 7

COOL-DOWN: Walk easily for 5 to 7 minutes, then stretch.

CALORIES USED: 310

COMMENTS

Be sure to repeat some of Workouts 1-5 before moving on to this Challenge Tempo at a faster pace. Take a minute to assess how far your fitness has come based on the speed and intensity you can now accomplish.

10 TREADMILL/CHALLENGE TEMPO WALK
TOTAL TIME: 50-55 minutes

WARM-UP: Walk for about 5 minutes at a slow pace (3.5-3.7 mph), stretch, then walk for another 2 minutes at a more moderate pace.

WORKOUT

Distance: 2-1/2 miles
Walking time: 34 minutes
Pace: 13- to 14-minute miles (4.3-4.6 mph)
Effort: 85-89% max HR; RPE 7

COOL-DOWN: Walk easily for 5 to 7 minutes, then stretch.

CALORIES USED: 290

COMMENTS

Take advantage of the control you have to increase your speed as you go. First mile: 4.3 mph. Second mile: 4.4 mph. Last half-mile: 4.6 mph. As you advance, you can increase each stage by another tenth of a mile in speed.

11

Red Zone

If Orange workouts are for advanced walkers, then Red workouts are for *very* advanced walkers—those perhaps dabbling their toes in competition and trying out the race walking gait, or who have jumped into weekend races with more emphasis on the hands of the watch and improving their time performance.

Whether you're already one of those athletic walkers or strive to be, these workouts will tantalize the speed lying latent within you. Although they can help groom speedy walking, these alone cannot be used for serious race walk training, if that is your goal. They are only an appetizer.

If you're serious about racing, training, and technique, you can find local race walking clubs by calling the national governing federation, USA Track & Field, based in Indianapolis, Indiana. A local club can direct you to coaches and racing camaraderie and can provide the judged races you might need or crave. Take note that race walkers serious about competition train much the same way runners do, so even running books with their discussions of different training seasons, various types of complex intervals, and race preparation can help you get started.

Meanwhile, here's a training teaser for the walking speed demons. In this chapter I'll introduce one workout (Threshold Intervals) and modify two others (Challenge Tempos and Long walks) that you got to know in previous chapters.

- **Threshold Intervals.** First, let's clarify the basis of this new workout. Your "lactate threshold" is the point at which your body suddenly says you're exercising too hard. When you reach that point, you have moved out of primarily aerobic metabolism, which uses oxygen and can keep you going nearly forever, into a higher percentage of anaerobic metabolism, which works without oxygen and can't go on forever.

  With a limited supply of oxygen, your body pushes the panic button and starts dumping more waste products, such as lactic acid, into your bloodstream to get you to stop exercising. Oxygen is what helps clear these waste products, so without oxygen they cannot be metabolized quickly enough to be cleared from your blood. The accumulation of waste products is what causes you to feel heavy and fatigued, and to slow down or stop.

  But with training you can move your threshold higher, allowing you to exercise at higher intensities and faster speeds without dumping excess lactic acid and while continuing to work more aerobically. To do that, however, you must find a speed that lets you train just below your threshold. Tickle at that threshold enough, and your body gives in and moves it higher. You respond by training a little harder, and the body again moves the threshold higher, and so continues the tag game.

  Without laboratory testing to pinpoint your exact threshold, you can only guess that it's about 80% to 85% of your age-predicted heart rate maximum, which you determined using the formula explained in the Part II introduction to the walking zones. If you are less fit your threshold may be below this range; if you are more fit, it will be at the higher end or perhaps above it. The threshold of a competitive athlete may extend up to 90% or 95%. You should work very hard during the intervals, which last from 1 to 2-1/2 miles each. Each Threshold Intervals workout includes two or three intervals, with short rests between. You could do one of these workouts once or twice a week as you advance.

This chapter also will encourage you to challenge yourself with longer workouts and longer races, from 10 kilometers (6.2 miles) up to half-marathons (13.1 miles). Walks will last from about 45 minutes up to 2-1/2 hours. Your perceived exertion will hit the high end, from 6 to 8, or between 80% and 95% of your maximum heart rate. During Challenge Tempo walks your heart rate and perceived exertion may go quite high, especially if you're participating in a local race. Proper training and preparation allow your body to handle these increases.

Red Zone Preview				
Workout	Description	Duration (minutes)	Distance (miles)	Intensity (% max HR/RPE)
1	Threshold Intervals	46-50	4	80-89/6-7
2	Threshold Intervals	46-50	4-1/2	80-89/6-7
3	Long walk	60	5	80-84/6
4	Long walk	84	7	80-84/6
5	Long walk	120-130	10	80-84/6
6	Long Tempo walk	69-72	6	80-89/6-7
7	Challenge Tempo walk	69-72	6.2	85-94/7-8
8	Challenge Tempo walk	102-112	9.3	85-94/7-8
9	Long Tempo walk	144-157	13.1	85-94/7-8
10	Treadmill/ Tempo walk	63-64	5	80-94/6-8

1

THRESHOLD INTERVALS
TOTAL TIME: 65-70 minutes

WARM-UP: Walk for about a mile at an easy pace, stretch, then walk for another 3 to 4 minutes at a more moderate pace. Pick up the speed in the last minute to a sprint pace. Let your heart rate drop to the easy pace level before starting.

WORKOUT

Distance: 4 miles

Walking time: 46-50 minutes

Pace: 11-1/2- to 13-minute miles for the fast intervals

Effort: 80-89% max HR; RPE 6-7

COOL-DOWN: Walk easily for a half-mile to a mile, then stretch.

CALORIES USED: 420

COMMENTS

This workout consists of three intervals. The first is 2 miles, the second and third are 1 mile each. Try to keep your pace less than 13-minute miles, averaging closer to 12-minute miles or less. After the first interval, rest 8 or 9 minutes by strolling around very easily, even 15-minute miles or less. After the second interval, rest by strolling 2 or 3 minutes. Perceived exertion and heart rate during the strolling rest should drop to equal your early warm-up levels. An active cool-down, where you continue to walk easily, is vital after such a hard workout to offset muscle soreness.

WORKOUT 2

THRESHOLD INTERVALS
TOTAL TIME: 75-80 minutes

2

WARM-UP: Walk for about a mile at an easy pace, stretch, then walk for another 3 to 4 minutes at a more moderate pace. Pick up the speed in the last minute to a sprint pace. Let your heart rate drop to the easy pace level before starting.

WORKOUT

Distance: 4-1/2 miles

Walking time: 46-50 minutes

Pace: 11- to 12-minute miles for the fast intervals

Effort: 80-89% max HR; RPE 6-7

COOL-DOWN: Walk easily for a half-mile to a mile, then stretch.

CALORIES USED: 495

COMMENTS

This workout consists of two intervals. The first is 2-1/2 miles at a 12-minute pace (or faster). Take a 10-minute rest while strolling around easily, then do another 2-mile interval at the same pace. Go back to Workout 1 if the second interval in this workout is too exhausting. Note: Try this on a treadmill if you're stuck inside— a 12-minute mile is 5 mph, an 11-minute mile is 5.5 mph.

WORKOUT 3

3

LONG WALK
TOTAL TIME: 80 minutes

WARM-UP: Walk for 7 to 10 minutes at an easy pace, stretch, then walk for another 3 to 4 minutes at a more moderate pace.

WORKOUT
Distance: 5 miles
Walking time: 60 minutes
Pace: 12-minute miles
Effort: 80-84% max HR; RPE 6

COOL-DOWN: Walk easily for a half-mile to a mile, then stretch.

CALORIES USED: 525

COMMENTS
Long walks in the Red zone hint at moderate Tempo walks. This and Workout 4 can be used liberally as good general workouts, filling in several times a week when you can't or don't feel like doing anything speedier. Be sure to keep the distance; feel free to slow down to a perceived exertion of 4 to 5 if you need to.

WORKOUT 4

LONG WALK
TOTAL TIME: 104 minutes

WARM-UP: Walk for 7 to 10 minutes at an easy pace, stretch, then walk for another 3 to 4 minutes at a more moderate pace.

WORKOUT
Distance: 7 miles
Walking time: 84 minutes
Pace: 12-minute miles
Effort: 80-84% max HR; RPE 6

COOL-DOWN: Walk easily for a half-mile to a mile, then stretch.

CALORIES USED: 735

COMMENTS
You should be able to accomplish the previous walk before adding 2 miles. Be sure to take a very easy walk or a rest day after this. Again, feel free to ease the pace on this to a perceived exertion of 4 to 5, if your body demands it to be able to accomplish the distance. With larger walks, the warm-up distance can be the first part of the workout distance if desired.

WORKOUT 5

5

LONG WALK
TOTAL TIME: 140 to 150 minutes

WARM-UP: Walk for 7 to 10 minutes at an easy pace, stretch, then walk for another 3 to 4 minutes at a more moderate pace; or simply start your walk slower, gradually picking up the pace.

WORKOUT
Distance: 10 miles
Walking time: 120-130 minutes
Pace: 12- to 13-minute miles
Effort: 80-84% max HR; RPE 6
Terrain: Flat, or add rolling hills

COOL-DOWN: Walk easily for a half-mile to a mile, then stretch.

CALORIES USED: 1,010 (up to 250 more with some hills)

COMMENTS
This will give you strength to complete a 10K comfortably. Keep the pace steady, slowing your speed and perceived exertion slightly if desired to finish the entire distance.

WORKOUT 6

LONG TEMPO WALK
TOTAL TIME: 85-90 minutes

6

WARM-UP: Walk for 7 to 10 minutes at an easy pace, stretch, then walk for another 3 to 4 minutes at a more moderate pace.

WORKOUT

Distance: 6 miles

Walking time: 69-72 minutes

Pace: 11- to 12-minute miles

Effort: 80-89% max HR; RPE 6-7

COOL-DOWN: Walk easily for a half-mile to a mile, then stretch.

CALORIES USED: 660

COMMENTS

Whereas Workout 5 gives you strength over the long haul, this one will develop a bit of speed. Let yourself work hard for the entire distance.

WORKOUT 7

CHALLENGE TEMPO WALK
TOTAL TIME: 85-95 minutes

WARM-UP: Walk for about a mile at an easy pace, stretch, then walk for another 3 to 4 minutes at a faster pace; or incorporate the warm-up into the first part of the workout by starting slowly.

WORKOUT

Distance: 10 kilometers (6.2 miles)
Walking time: 69-72 minutes
Pace: 11- to 11-1/2-minute miles
Effort: 85-94% max HR; RPE 7-8

COOL-DOWN: Walk easily for a half-mile to a mile, then stretch.

CALORIES USED: 680

COMMENTS

Find a local 10K run for this workout. The energy of the pack will help keep you going. Pick one that offers "split times," meaning there are markers every mile and, most likely, someone calling out times. That'll help you keep your pace. Don't start out too fast. And don't worry about being last. You'll be surprised how slow some joggers run.

WORKOUT 8

CHALLENGE TEMPO WALK
TOTAL TIME: 115-130 minutes

8

WARM-UP: Walk for about a mile at an easy pace, stretch, then walk for another 3 to 4 minutes at a faster pace; or incorporate the warm-up into the first part of the workout by starting slowly.

WORKOUT

Distance: 15 kilometers (9.3 miles)
Walking time: 102-112 minutes
Pace: 11- to 12-minute miles
Effort: 85-94% max HR; RPE 7-8

COOL-DOWN: Walk easily for a half-mile to a mile, then stretch.

CALORIES USED: 940

COMMENTS

Look for a 15K weekend race, which will be harder to find than the omnipresent 10Ks. If need be, substitute a 12K (7.4 miles) running race or find your own route on a local marked trail and note your time. You can also complete a 10K race then keep walking for another 3 miles after the finish. Forget about hard workouts for a week to 10 days after this workout to give your body a chance to recover.

WORKOUT 9

9

LONG TEMPO WALK
TOTAL TIME: 160-175 minutes

WARM-UP: Walk for about a mile at an easy pace, stretch, then walk for another 3 to 4 minutes at a faster pace; or incorporate the warm-up into the first part of the race by starting slowly and gradually speeding up.

WORKOUT

Distance: Half-marathon (13.1 miles)
Walking time: 144-157 minutes
Pace: 12- to 13-minute miles
Effort: 85-94% max HR; RPE 7-8

COOL-DOWN: Walk easily for a half-mile to a mile, then stretch.

CALORIES USED: 1,325

COMMENTS

Find a friend to accompany you on this long one. Remember to drink water and carbohydrate beverages provided along the route (or take your own) because your muscles will start craving energy after about 90 minutes. If you can't find a convenient half-marathon, then try a 20-kilometer race (12.4 miles). You'll feel empowered after you complete this distance.

WORKOUT 10

TREADMILL/TEMPO WALK
TOTAL TIME: 80-85 minutes

10

WARM-UP: Walk for about a mile at an easy pace (4 mph), stretch, then walk for another 3 to 4 minutes at a faster pace (4.5 mph).

WORKOUT
Distance: 5 miles
Walking time: 63-64 minutes
Pace: 11-1/2- to 14-minute miles
Effort: 80-94% max HR; RPE 6-8

COOL-DOWN: Walk easily for a half-mile to a mile, then stretch.

CALORIES USED: 505

COMMENTS
Use the treadmill's exact speed control on this one to create a "pyramid" walk—graduating up, then back down in speed. First mile, 4.3 mph; second, 4.6; third, 5.0; fourth, 5.2; fifth and last, 5.0 (or 4.6 if you need a break). Create your own speed pyramids too, using this as a model.

PART III

TRAINING BY THE WORKOUT ZONES

Now you'll let the rubber hit the road—or, rather, the tennies hit the trail. Here's where you put together everything you've learned in Part I, with all the ingredients of the walking workouts detailed in Part II. The right combination, plus discipline and patience, will let you reach or maintain your personal level of fitness and explore your walking potential.

Notice I say not *goal* but *potential*. That's because a goal can be too limiting and too specific. Your potential, on the other hand, can be bottomless, and it is based entirely on your abilities and your needs, which can change from day to day, from year to year, from mood to mood.

Approaches to Walking

The walking programs fit into three categories, each with specific demands and characteristics. Choose workout programs that fit your style or needs, which of course may change at any time!

- **Beginning/easy.** This fits many people. You may be new to exercise and want to lose weight or lower your blood cholesterol levels. You may have been injured and need to ease back slowly into exercise. Perhaps you used to exercise, haven't for years, and would like to start again. You probably don't expect to walk more than 1 or 2 miles, two or three times a week, with an occasional easy weekend walk up to 3 miles. Many of your walks will be at a strolling pace. Time and pace won't be a concern to you.
- **Frequent/moderate.** Consider yourself part of this category if you walk three or four times a week, perhaps covering 3 or 4 miles each time. You may satisfy your fitness needs with that alone. But you might also be an exerciser who uses walking to fill gaps between other activities—working out at a health club, taking aerobics or martial arts classes, riding a bicycle, even running. Either way, walking is an important part of your regimen or may be your entire fitness program. You usually participate in brisk walks with occasional athletic walking.
- **Advanced/intense.** You, my friend, are a serious walker. This is your sport and you are very dedicated. If you miss a couple of days, you feel guilty, right? Your walking workouts average 4 to 6 miles, 5 or 6 days a week, with some longer jaunts here and there. Perhaps you already compete in walking, or you've thought about it. And you probably already keep one eye on your watch as you walk. Most of your walks are athletic walks with hints of race walking.

Program Selection

Although the book's workout zones are laid out in ascending order, the walks are to be mixed and matched. Most walkers will select from several zones to meet individual needs or time constraints.

A beginner may stick mostly to Green and Blue zones and only dabble in the Purples. Intermediate walkers might find satisfaction from Purple and Yellow zone walks, with occasional forays into Oranges for a new challenge or Blues for a quick and easy noontime break. An advanced walker might choose from any number of workouts, ranging from primarily Oranges and Reds, to Purples, and even a Green or Blue thrown in for the day after a really intense workout.

The combinations are endless. They are meant to be fully explored and fully enjoyed. The examples given are only a springboard, intended to introduce you to the concept of using this book as your workout smorgasbord.

Now pull on those rubber soles and get ready to hit the road. I'll show you in Part III how to set up a program and outline samples for each category. I'll also help you decide what sample program to follow if you want to use the samples as a guide.

12

Setting Up Your Program

Pulling together the parts to a walking program shouldn't be complicated. That's one of the joys of walking and probably one of the reasons you've chosen this as a key part of your activity. Still, some guidelines must be considered for a safe and effective program, whether you're young or old, competitive or moderate, a former jock or a beginning fitness exerciser.

Listen to Your Body

The human body is a smart machine, if only we'd pay attention to the subtle and not-so-subtle messages it sends us daily. The more you exercise, the more you'll find yourself in tune with those signals. And that's good. Taking heed can mean the difference between getting hurt and walking injury-free, getting sick and staying healthy.

Listen to the little aches, pains, and twinges in your joints and muscles. If something aches for more than 2 or 3 days, you probably should consult a doctor. Other signals are important too, because your ability to exercise fluctuates based on fatigue, stress, your previous workout, illness, your workload, emotions, and even weather.

All those can affect your body's engine—the heart. Learn to take your resting heart rate (before you get out of bed in the morning) and to take note of your pulse before, during, and after workouts. If your resting heart rate is 10% higher than normal, consider taking the day off or slipping in a very easy workout. If your pulse is higher than normal before a workout, take it easy. If it doesn't recover as quickly afterward, plan a rest the next day. And speaking of rest . . .

Easy Does It

Eagerness will take you far, but doing too much too soon can bring on soreness, injury, and an early end to good intentions. Two rules apply:

1. The 10% rule. Increase your mileage by no more than about 10% from one week to the next. If you have to take some time off (say because of illness or for a vacation), start back at a lower level and build again.
2. The hard–easy rule. Alternate every hard workout with rest or an easy workout to allow your muscles to recuperate and heal. A hard workout means either faster or longer than normal *for you*. For the beginner or easy walker, the hard–easy rule means walking only every other day. If you're a moderate walker, either take a day off or do an easy workout after a hard one. And an advanced walker should rotate long or fast walks with 1 or 2 days of easy ones.

Step 1: Setting Your Pace

Deciding what distances you can walk and at what speed takes you back to the assessments in chapter 3.

The first assessment was a checklist about your current fitness and health status. Your answers placed you in one of three groups: high, average, or low.

Now cross-check that rating with your result in the walking fitness test where you paced off a quick mile. Your walking time ranked in one of three categories, from high to low.

A "high" rating in the first assessment will most likely correspond with a "high" in the walk; an "average" will match up with a "moderate" in the walk; and a "low" will match up with a "low" in the walk.

If your results were this clear-cut, the following table shows you which walking program will be right for you.

But if the two didn't mesh so neatly, use your rating for the 1-mile walk to guide you into a walking program. Your mile time demonstrated what you can really do when you're putting one foot in front of the other.

Remember, however, this is only a guide. If you find yourself on the border between levels, be conservative to start and follow the easier program. Dabble gradually in the higher zones until you find what's right for you. Feel free to mix and match workouts if you find yourself

Choosing Your Program		
Walking program	**Overall health**	**Walk test**
Advanced/intense	High	High
Frequent/moderate	Average	Moderate
Beginning/easy	Low	Low

somewhere in the middle. That's the beauty of six zones—there will be workouts to match every tiny variation in personal fitness levels and daily energy swings. Always, as I first said, listen to your body.

Another part of the assessment of your level must come from within. If your ranking placed you in the advanced level, but you have no desire to move that fast, then move back to more moderate programs. The same goes for those ranked in the moderate level; step back to easier programs if that will fulfill your walking wishes.

Feel free to retake the 1-mile timed walk test every month or so to see how you're progressing and to get confidence to pump up your program.

© John Huet

Listen to your body—it will help you pick appropriate workouts.

EVALUATING YOUR TIME

Hours in a week   **168**

Sleeping	_____ per day × 7 = –_____
Personal hygiene	_____ per day × 7 = –_____
Eating	_____ per day × 7 = –_____
Work/commuting	_____ per day × 7 = –_____
Family commitments	_____ per day × 7 = –_____
School/homework	_____ per day × 7 = –_____
General tasks	_____ per day × 7 = –_____
Shopping	_____ per day × 7 = –_____
Recreation/relaxation	_____ per day × 7 = –_____
Other	_____ per day × 7 = –_____

Total   _____

Hours for exercise   _____

Step 2: Choosing Your Schedule

For most of us, life's time constraints hamper what we'd like to do, what we know we should do, and what we really can do. So take a moment to evaluate your time. (This tool gives an amazingly realistic assessment of your life's demands. Redo it as your schedule changes.)

We've all got 168 hours in a week. Record the time you spend on all your duties and requirements, from sleeping to commuting to driving the kids to ballgames, and subtract each from the 168. Be sure to add in 10 hours or so for those pesky little General Tasks such as stopping at the dry cleaners and the bank.

Do you have hours left for walking? Great—you'll have no problems reaching your personal potential. Or is your time account in the red before you even get to exercise? Look at how you allot your time and decide if you can steal an hour or so from another category for exercise time. Do you have a goal of walking 6 days a week for an hour but now see that you only have 2 free hours? You must decide where your priorities are and perhaps start with less walking time as you learn to rejuggle the demands in your schedule.

Try to get in at least three 20-minute walks a week. As you progress, you can aim for three to five weekly exercise sessions of 20 to 60 minutes (as recommended by the American College of Sports Medicine for quality cardiovascular improvement). But any activity, even going a few blocks with a friend, can help improve your health.

Step 3: Selecting Your Workouts

Know yourself and how you fit into the three levels we outlined earlier. Recognize what you want from a walking program, whether simply strolling 1 easy mile three times a week, briskly striding 15-minute miles for 45 minutes four times a week, or being able to breeze through an athletic 10- or 11-minute mile without huffing and panting.

Select from the sample programs in the next chapter accordingly.

© F-Stock/David Epperson

Progress comes daily if you pay attention to your body.

13

Sample Walking Programs

Here you will find six 4-week programs, geared toward the three types of walkers detailed earlier—two beginning/easy sample programs, two frequent/moderate samples, and two advanced/intense samples. Each sample shows workout days and rest days. On workout days, the colors refer to the different zones and the numbers refer to the workouts within these zones. Whatever program you follow, it will improve your health and fitness as well as hone your walking style and technique.

Beginning/Easy Walking Program

Many beginners will go directly to Blue workouts and may be able to tackle Purple workouts in no time. Green workouts are very easy and will suit you best if you're completely new to movement or haven't enjoyed regular activity in many years.

As a beginner, you will be walking two or three times a week, making sure to take at least 1 day off between walks. You will probably cover 2 to 6 miles a week.

The first sample program is for the newly active person. It is designed to ease you into walking slowly, mixing small amounts of walking with lots of rest.

WEEK 1	Su	M	Tu	W	Th	F	Sa
	1		3			3	

WEEK 2	Su	M	Tu	W	Th	F	Sa
		3		1		4	

WEEK 3	Su	M	Tu	W	Th	F	Sa
	4			5		2	

WEEK 4	Su	M	Tu	W	Th	F	Sa
	7		8			9	

A walk at any pace is good for your health.

© F-Stock/Kristen Olenick

The next sample program is slightly harder than the first, adding longer and slightly more intense walks. Although it's also called beginning, the sample I've laid out is not for someone who is unprepared or who has never exercised. You must already have at least several weeks of walking under your belt and be able to walk a mile before attempting to follow a schedule like the one below.

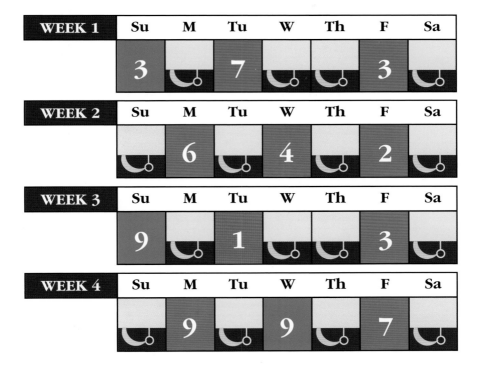

Frequent/Moderate Walking Program

Most frequent walkers will find their needs completely met by the intermediate Purple and Yellow zone workouts. Still, you might want to try an occasional Orange walk, or slip in an easy Blue jaunt as a rest.

You will walk three or four times a week. A rest day is still important after a walk, but you might walk 2 days in a row, with the second day being quite easy. You will cover 10 to 15 miles a week, and the more advanced frequent walkers will be able to complete weekend "fun walks" of 2 or 3 miles.

This first sample program will meet your all-around exercise needs.

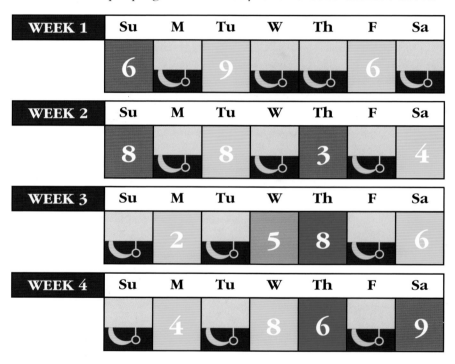

The second sample focuses on building strength through a program of Long and Tempo walks from mostly the Yellow zone. These leave out Speed Play and concentrate on Steady walking at different speeds. Advanced walkers can also use 1 or 2 weeks of such a program when they feel the need for simpler workouts.

WEEK 1	Su	M	Tu	W	Th	F	Sa
	8	6		7		6	

WEEK 2	Su	M	Tu	W	Th	F	Sa
	8		4		9		1

WEEK 3	Su	M	Tu	W	Th	F	Sa
	8		6	9		7	

WEEK 4	Su	M	Tu	W	Th	F	Sa
	8	3		9	7	8	

© F-Stock/Caroline Wood

Picking up the speed brings quicker fitness gains.

Advanced/Intense Walking Program

As an advanced walker, even if you never compete formally, you often keep one eye on your watch and are continually competing with yourself. You'll choose mostly from Orange and Red zones. Still, don't neglect mixing in longer and more moderate Yellow workouts for variety. With the right mix, you'll improve your personal performances and be ready for many weekend 10K walks.

Advanced walkers don't miss more than 1 or 2 days a week, and they have the strength to walk on back-to-back days. But you should still be certain that those back-to-back workouts aren't both hard ones. You'll easily cover 20 to 30 miles a week.

Our first sample is a varied program mixing most types of walks, from Easy to Speed Play to Challenge Tempo.

WEEK 1	Su	M	Tu	W	Th	F	Sa
	9	4	9	3	8	(rest)	1

WEEK 2	Su	M	Tu	W	Th	F	Sa
	3	5	(rest)	4	6	2	3

WEEK 3	Su	M	Tu	W	Th	F	Sa
	(rest)	1	9	2	(rest)	4	3

WEEK 4	Su	M	Tu	W	Th	F	Sa
	6	(rest)	9	2	(rest)	9	4

The second advanced walking program focuses solely on building speed with workouts that concentrate on weekly Threshold Interval and Tempo walks, with Speed Play jaunts tossed in to get your feet moving faster. This type of program can be followed for 1 to 4 weeks at a time, with your 4th week allowing a decrease in mileage—but not intensity— to give your body a rest.

WEEK 1	Su	M	Tu	W	Th	F	Sa
	2	1	3	2		1	9

WEEK 2	Su	M	Tu	W	Th	F	Sa
	5	4	6	3		2	8

WEEK 3	Su	M	Tu	W	Th	F	Sa
	9		1	1	2	2	4

WEEK 4	Su	M	Tu	W	Th	F	Sa
	4	3	6		1	7	6

Give your walk an intense push for high aerobic fitness.

Treading on a Mill

The sample workout programs incorporate workouts intended to head outdoors. But I've also designed one walk in each zone (Workout 10) for a treadmill. One of the joys of walking is getting out from inside four walls, but sometimes circumstances—weather, convenience, travel demands, kids that need watching—will mean you'll want to stay inside on a treadmill.

And there's nothing wrong with treadmill workouts. They can actually have benefits that outdoor walking doesn't provide. You can control exactly how far and how fast you go, and you can incorporate hills at whim, as often or as steep as you want. Using a treadmill also lets you walk before or after dark when it might be unsafe outdoors. And you can even watch TV or otherwise distract yourself on those days when you don't much feel like walking.

All the workouts in the book can be adapted for a treadmill; just translate the minutes per mile to miles per hour (see the table on p. 53). Gradual or rolling hills would be about a 3-5% incline. Use an incline on which you're still comfortable walking naturally, with your arms bent or extended at your sides. If you have to hang on to the bar to keep up with the speed, the incline is too steep. Whether you're treading on rubber or on pavement, the recommendations for warm-up, stretching, and cooldown all apply.

To equate more accurately your speed on a treadmill to speed in the open air, you need to add a 1% incline. Because you have no wind resistance indoors, the 1% approximately balances the energy requirements.

Indoors or out, other types of movement are important to a well-rounded fitness program. In the next chapter I'll talk about the components you'll want to add to your walking workouts.

14

Cross-Training

Cross-training is just a fancy term for mixing up your fitness activities. Think of it as "fitness grazing." It should be fun and keep your body healthier and your mind more alert. More and more people are discovering cross-training. According to a 1992 national poll conducted for *Outside* magazine, the number of Americans who participate in more than one activity is expected to jump in 10 years by 73%—outpacing even the impressively increasing numbers of walkers. Maybe you should be one of those people.

Why Cross-Train?

Even as a walking aficionado, you should dabble in other activities for several reasons:

1. You will strengthen and tone muscles that walking doesn't target. Walking requires concentrated use of the muscles in the back of the leg, which can cause strength and flexibility imbalances. Cross-training can resolve those imbalances.
2. Multiple activities can generate added enthusiasm for exercise. Trying out a smattering of activities will keep your mind and your body interested in exercise and will promote lifelong participation.
3. It's good to have activities to fall back on in case of an injury. If you need—or are forced into taking—a few days or a few months off from walking, you'll know how to substitute other activities so you can maintain your health, fitness, and vitality.

Aerobic Cross-Training

Walking may be your number 1 choice for cardiovascular fitness. That's great because it's so adaptable. But other activities can round out your exercise menu. As usual, aim for a minimum of 20 minutes of any activity.

Don't limit yourself to the activities I've highlighted here, although these offer certain advantages as an adjunct to walking.

Bicycling

A bicycle can offer freedom to see areas your feet can't take you. The movement can also be a relief from walking's repetitive heel–toe routine.

A great leg strengthener, the cycling action has no impact on the joints and uses more of the muscle in the front of your thigh (quadriceps) than walking does. And you can still get outdoors and watch the world go by.

Thirty minutes of cycling at a steady 15 mph will use nearly the same amount of energy as walking for 30 minutes at 4.5 mph.

Aerobics

Since its "dancey" beginnings, aerobics has evolved into a wide variety of group-exercise classes. There is something to match every taste and every coordination level, including low-impact, step training, circuit and interval classes, funk, and slide conditioning.

Not only are classes held indoors (a great alternative to walks in inclement weather), but one session can work out your whole body. Trendy music adds a fun element, too. Don't overlook water aerobics or aqua step classes as a possibility.

Of course, you can also pop a tape into your VCR and turn your living room into your private studio for a quick workout at your own convenience.

Most sessions will include 30 to 35 minutes of aerobics plus 10 minutes of warm-up and stretch and 5 to 10 minutes of cool-down and stretch. As with cycling, 30 minutes of low-impact aerobics, not including warm-up and cool-down, will use about the same number of calories as walking 30 minutes at 4.5 mph.

Swimming

Swimming uses more muscle in the upper body, in contrast to walking's nearly exclusive use of lower body muscles. It also promotes flexibility where walking, like other upright activities, tends to tighten.

It's not that walkers need a break from impact, but swimming's fluid cushion eliminates any slight element of pounding or strain from gravity. Immersion in water can soothe body as well as mind, adding peaceful alternatives to street walks.

You'll have to swim laps steadily for 30 minutes for a workout equivalent to walking 30 minutes at 4 mph.

Stationary Equipment

The incredible variety in indoor exercise equipment now available leaves an exerciser with no excuse for not finding something enjoyable.

Depending on your needs as a walker, you can choose equipment at a club or for your home to emphasize walking muscles (treadmills or stairclimbers), to emphasize opposing muscles (bicycles, rowing machines), or to train the whole body (ladderlike climbers, cross-country ski machines, dual-action bicycles). Indoor workouts let you distract yourself with television, movies, or reading—or simply offer a change of pace.

On most indoor equipment, you will feel as if you're working harder than you would during a walk. Let your body tell you how long the workout should be. 20-30 minutes on most of the equipment mentioned above will give you a good workout.

Substitute other activities occasionally for muscle balance.

Spice Up Your Walking

Walking itself can be transformed into a cross-training routine by adding equipment, diversifying your route, or changing your walking style.

Pole Walking

Much like cross-country skiing, but without skis or snow, walking using poles with special rubber tips can use a third to a half more calories than regular walking. Plus, poling along demands more from back, chest, and arm muscles.

Pole walking can increase calorie use and strengthen upper-body muscles.

Retro Walking

This odd-sounding activity is no more than walking backward. Retro walking demands more energy than forward walking, reduces impact to near zero, and changes the pattern of muscle use to increase the demand on the quadriceps in the front of your thigh. Try short stretches of this (with one eye over your shoulder!) on flat trails or uncrowded tracks.

Run-Walk

Maybe you like the feeling of bobbing along in a jog, but you don't like the impact. Try interspersing your walks with short runs of 1 or 2 minutes.

A more advanced walker can turn the runs into short sprints; an intermediate walker can make the run slow and easy and use it as a rest from fast walking. Beginners should stick with walking.

Outdoor Circuit

So you don't have time to get to a health club? Transform the outdoors into your own gym by looking at variations in the environment as places to challenge your muscles.

Do step-ups on curbs or low benches. Walls or fences are great for push-ups. Try triceps dips on planters or benches. Jump up and touch signs or ceilings. Hop over low obstacles. In between all those, keep on walking.

You can even carry rubber tubes or bands to add resistance exercises to your personalized routine. Walking with hand weights (addressed in chapter 2) isn't worth the potential for injury. The same goes for ankle weights, which also unsafely throw off your body mechanics and can strain your joints.

Stretch and Strengthen

No fitness program can be well rounded without exercises for flexibility and muscle strength.

Flexibility exercises should be the unquestioned finish of every walk, with additional stretching on rest days. Think about doing casual or impromptu stretches, such as a back stretch while sitting at your desk or a calf stretch while waiting in a grocery check-out line.

If you don't stretch, walking, like any activity, will slowly tighten the muscles you use—in your buttocks (gluteal group), the backs of your thighs (hamstrings), and your calves. It's important to follow the flexibility exercises I detailed in chapter 5 to continue walking injury-free.

Because of the vigorous arm swing, walking tones upper body muscles more than running (good distance running form demands carrying the arms more passively). That's not enough, though, to keep bones healthy and muscles strong for the rest of your life's demands.

Exercises to strengthen muscles need not be complicated or expensive. Health clubs certainly offer all the equipment you need to target walking's underused muscles in the chest, back, and shoulders as well as to strengthen the well-used muscles in the legs. But abdominal exercises and push-ups can be done on your living room floor, and pulling on inexpensive rubber surgical tubing is a fine substitute for using a weight machine to condition muscles in the back, chest, arms, and legs.

As you fine-tune your overall fitness program, you'll want to try to find time for two muscle-toning sessions a week, as recommended by the American College of Sports Medicine. Target large muscle groups from head to toe. Such a toning routine doesn't require more than 20 or 25 minutes, although you can always do more if you want.

Monitoring your mood is a vital part of maintaining progress. In the last chapter, I'll talk about how to keep your motivation up and evaluate your progress.

15

Charting Your Progress

If you look at the black-and-white numbers of time and distance, then walking is one of many activities in which progress can be measured precisely. In this chapter, you'll learn about measurement and log-keeping—a vital part of any fitness program—but first I need to talk about mental progress.

The program laid out in *Fitness Walking* is founded on two promises from you, the walker:

- **Honesty.** You must always be true to yourself in assessing your personal ability, energy level, and needs, using only *you* as a yardstick, not a neighbor or friend. No walk is too slow, too little, or inadequate in any way. Every movement is a building block—accept it for what it is.
- **Diligence.** Stick-to-it-iveness is essential. Don't give up, no matter what. Fitness takes time, whether you're going from a sedentary lifestyle to 3-day-a-week walks or from brisk walking to serious power walking. Your body needs time to adjust, to build muscle, to learn to use fat more efficiently, and to increase lung and heart strength.

What is progress in a fitness program? Progress is about looking over the edge into the unknown chasm of human potential and depth of character, then jumping. It is a tale of exploring what your body can do, at whatever fitness level you choose, then trying it.

Making exercise a regular part of your life takes at least 6 weeks, and up to 6 months to become a real habit. For a beginner, making it to the 6-month mark is true progress. For more intermediate and advanced walkers, putting in additional effort to advance farther is progress. Exercise will become a real inspirational activity that will alter your mood from bad to good, your stress from high to nonexistent.

Evaluating Your Progress

Nonetheless, measurements must be made if you want to compare your workouts today with those from last week or last year. Make a copy of the training log on page 156 of this book. Use it to record your workouts and keep track of your progress. Good things to make note of in the comments section include the location of your walk, the weather, and how you felt.

Evaluate your progress three ways:

- **Time.** You can retake the 1-mile walking test at any time (preferably not more than once a month) and compare your time with previous 1-mile walks. In your log book, observe how long it takes you to cover certain distances. Are you moving faster? Note, too, which zones most of your workouts come from. The more intense the color, the faster and longer the workout. That's progress.
- **Feelings.** You'll notice a space in the sample log to jot down a couple of words about how you felt. Were your legs heavy or light? Were they sore or relaxed? Did the workout feel easy or as if the whole thing were uphill? Maybe you're going faster and farther, but it feels easier. All this relates to perceived exertion. Compare how you perceived your body during similar workouts in different weeks, as well as your rating of perceived exertion.
- **Physical signs.** Your body will let you know what's going on— listen to it. Your resting heart rate is one concrete measure. Take it and record it often. Usually, as someone gets more fit, the resting heart rate goes down. If it is suddenly higher than normal by 5 or 10 beats, that can signify overtraining, fatigue, stress, or even an impending illness. Take heed and take a break.

If you've had your body fat tested, test it again and note the change. A scale is not a good judge because your body weight might stay the same or even go up, although you lose fat and your clothes fit looser with consistent exercise. That's because muscle weighs more than fat.

What about your blood tests? Your blood cholesterol, low-density lipoprotein, and triglyceride levels will likely go down. No matter what your body weight does, this is progress toward better health.

Sleep patterns will improve. You'll fall asleep quicker, rest more soundly, and awaken more refreshed when you exercise. You'll also have more energy during the day.

Walking can be such a peaceful activity, at any speed. So today I proudly correct hotel clerks and associates when they ask if I'm going for a run. Nope, I'm going for my walk, I say. And I hold up my head proudly as I stride off for my workout.

Take the challenge to excel within your range of ability, or challenge yourself to push that range just a little. Progress in walking is about the journey, not the end, because there is no end. The journey is what feeds the mind and body.

Keep on walking, and you too will correct family, friends, and colleagues with pride as you continue your journey: "No, I'm going for a walk."

© F-Stock/Caroline Wood

As you progress, remember, *you* are the only yardstick for measuring your success.

Date	Pulse / Weight		Workout zone and #	Distance	Time	Comments
Su						
M						
Tu						
W						
Th						
F						
Sa						

Summary _____

Index

A

Adductor stretch, 44
Advanced/intense programs, 130, 142-143
Aerobic activities, for cross-training, 148
Age factors, 4, 27
American College of Sports Medicine, 135, 151
American Sports Data, 4
Ankle movement, 34
Arch supports, 16
Arm position and movement, 35-37, 39
Athletic walking, definition of, 10

B

Backaches, walking errors and, 38
Back stretch, 47
Beginning/easy programs, 130, 137-139
Benefits of walking, 5-8, 154-155
Bicycling, 148
Blue zone workouts
    basic guidelines, 67-68
    preview, 68
    specific instructions, 69-78
Body composition
    benefits of walking for, 5
    for evaluating progress, 154
Body weight. *See* Weight, body
Bones, 6-7
Borg, Gunnar, 51
Brisk walking, definition of, 10
Buttocks stretch, 44

C

Calf stretch, 46
Caloric cost, 52
Cardiovascular fitness/health
    assessment of, 26
    benefits of walking for, 5
Challenge tempo walks
    definition and guidelines, 103-104
    orange zone, 110-114
    red zone, 124-125
    treadmill, 114
Charting progress, 153-156
Circuit training, 151
Clothing, 7, 16-18, 19-20, 21, 22
Cold weather, 21, 23
Color-coding of workouts, 49-50
Cooling down
    basic guidelines, 42-43, 53
    stretches for, 43-48

Cooper Institute for Aerobics Research, 30
Costs, of equipment, 15, 19-20
Cross-training, 147-152

D

Distances for workouts
    for advanced/intense programs, 130, 142
    for beginning/easy programs, 130, 137
    blue zone, 67, 68
    for frequent/moderate programs, 130, 140
    green zone, 55, 56
    orange zone, 103, 104
    purple zone, 79, 80
    recording of, 156
    red zone, 116, 117
    techniques for measuring, 52-53
    yellow zone, 91, 92
Dress. *See* Clothing; Shoes
Duration of workouts
    blue zone, 67, 68
    general recommendations, 134-135
    green zone, 55, 56
    orange zone, 103, 104
    purple zone, 79, 80
    red zone, 116, 117
    yellow zone, 91, 92

E

Easy programs, 130, 137-139
Easy walks
    blue zone, 69-71
    definition and guidelines, 55
    green zone, 55-61
Elbow movement, 36, 39
Endurance. *See* Cardiovascular fitness/health; Muscular endurance
Equipment, 7, 13-20, 149
    clothing, 7, 16-18, 19-20, 21, 22
    costs of, 15, 19-20
    miscellaneous accessories, 18, 20, 24
    shoes, 7, 13, 14-16, 19
    for stationary exercise, 149
Etiquette, on tracks, 53
Exercise equipment, 149. *See also* Treadmill walks
Exercises. *See also* Stretching exercises
    cross-training, 147-152
    for muscle strength, 6, 151-152
Eyewear, 18

F

Fifteen kilometer (15K) races, 125

Fitness assessment, 25-31
    for evaluating progress, 133, 154
    one-mile walking test, 30-31, 132, 133, 154
    for pace selection, 132
    questionnaires, 8, 26-29, 132
    reasons for, 25
Flexibility. See Stretching exercises
Foot movement, 34-35
Footwear, 7, 13, 14-16, 19
Form for walking, 33-39
Frequency of workouts
    for advanced/intense programs, 130,
        142-143
    for beginning/easy programs, 130, 137-139
    for frequent/moderate programs, 130,
        140-141
    general recommendations, 134
Frequent/moderate programs, 130, 140-141
Frostbite, 21

G
Glasses (eyewear), 18
Gloves, 18, 20
Goal pace, definition of, 92
Goals, vs. potential, 129
Green zone workouts
    basic guidelines, 55-56
    preview, 56
    specific instructions, 57-66

H
Half-marathon races, 126
Hamstring stretch, 43
Hand position, 37
Hand weights, 18
Hard-easy rule, 132
Hats and headgear, 17, 20, 22
Health history/screening, 26-29. See also
        Fitness assessment
Heart-rate monitor, 18
Heart rate (pulse rate). See also Intensity of
        workouts
    for evaluating progress, 154
    for fitness assessment, 27
    for measuring workout intensity, 50-51
    for program planning, 131-132
Heatstroke, 22
Heel supports, 16
Heel-toe technique, 34-35
Hip movement, 35, 38
Hip stretch, 44
Hot weather, 22
Humidity, 22
Hypothermia, 21

I
Iliotibial band stretch, 45
Illnesses, and fitness assessment, 27
Imbalances, muscle, 6
Immune system, 7
Injuries. See also Safety
    fitness assessment and, 26
    prevention of, 9, 16, 103, 132
Intense programs, 130, 142-143

Intensity of workouts
    blue zone, 50, 67, 68
    color-coding explained, 50
    green zone, 50, 55, 56
    orange zone, 50, 103, 104
    purple zone, 50, 79, 80
    red zone, 50, 116, 117
    techniques for measuring, 50-51
    yellow zone, 1, 50, 92
Intervals, threshold, 116, 118-119

J
Jackets, 18

K
Ketchum, Brad, 5
Knee movement, for race walking, 37, 38

L
Lactate threshold, 30, 116
Location for walking, 23, 53
Log (recordkeeping form), 154, 156
Long tempo walks, 123, 126
Long walks
    blue zone, 76-77
    definition and guidelines, 67-68
    red zone, 120-123, 126
    treadmill, 102
    yellow zone, 98-102
Lower back stretch, 47
Lower body, and walking technique, 34-35,
        37-38

M
Marathon race walking, 126
Maximal oxygen uptake ($\dot{V}O_2$max), 30-31
Maximum heart rate, 50-51. See also
        Intensity of workouts
Mental progress, 153
Mittens, 18
Moderate programs, 130, 140-141
Muscle imbalances, 6
Muscular endurance, 5
Muscular strength. See Strength

N
National Sporting Goods Association, 3
Nieman, David, 7

O
Off-road shoes, 15
Olympic Games, 38
One-mile walking test, 30-31, 132, 133, 154
Orange zone workouts
    basic guidelines, 103-104
    preview, 104
    specific instructions, 105-114
Orthotics, 16
Osteoporosis, 6-7
Outerwear, 18, 21
Outside magazine, 147
Overstriding, 35, 38

P
Pace for workouts. See also Speed for
        workouts

for challenge tempo walks, 103-104
for easy walks, 55
goal pace defined, 92
guidelines for selection of, 132-133
for long walks, 68
recording of, 156
for specific zones, 56, 80, 92
for steady walks, 56
techniques for measuring, 53
for tempo walks, 79
Pants, 17, 18
PAR-Q & You (Physical Activity Readiness
    Questionnaire), 8, 26
Perceived exertion, 51. *See also* Intensity of
    workouts
Petroleum jelly, 18
Physical Activity Readiness Questionnaire
    (PAR-Q & You), 8, 26
Pole walking, 150
Posture, 33, 35
Potential, definition of, 129
Programs for walking. *See also* Schedules for
    walking
    advanced/intense, 130, 142-143
    beginning/easy, 130, 137-139
    charting progress of, 153-156
    frequent/moderate, 130, 140-141
    guidelines for selection of, 130, 132-133
    guidelines for setting up, 131-135
    safety considerations, 131-132
    types defined, 130
Progress charting, 153-156
Pulse rate. *See* Heart rate (pulse rate)
Purple zone
    basic guidelines, 79-80
    preview, 80
    specific instructions, 81-90

Q
Quadriceps stretch, 45

R
Race walking
    definition of, 9
    history of, 38
    joining organizations for, 115
    shoes for, 15
    specific types of races, 124-126
    technique for, 37-38
    workouts for, 118-127
Rainwear, 18
Rating of perceived exertion (RPE), 51. *See
    also* Intensity of workouts
Readiness questionnaires, 8, 26-29, 132. *See
    also* Fitness assessment
Recordkeeping, 153-156
Recovery/rest, 80, 91, 103, 132
Red zone workouts
    basic guidelines, 115-116
    preview, 117
    specific instructions, 118-127
Relative humidity, 22

Rest/recovery, 80, 91, 103, 132
Retro walking, 150
Rippe, James, 5, 9
RPE (rating of perceived exertion), 51. *See
    also* Intensity of workouts
Run-walk, 151

S
Safety. *See also* Fitness assessment
    basic rules for, 23-24
    cooling down for, 42-43, 53
    injury prevention, 9, 16, 103, 132
    location and, 23
    personal stereos and, 18, 24
    program planning and, 131-132
    rest/recovery for, 80, 91, 103, 132
    shoes for, 16
    for stretches, 43
    traffic and, 18, 23-24
    walking errors and, 38-39
    warming up for, 41-42, 53
    weather and, 21-23
Schedules for walking. *See also* Programs
    for walking
    for advanced/intense programs, 130,
        142-143
    basic guidelines, 134-135
    for beginning/easy programs, 130,
        137-139
    for frequent/moderate programs, 130,
        140-141
    safety considerations, 131-132
Shin stretch, 46
Shirts, 17, 20, 22
Shoes, 7, 13, 14-16, 19
Shorts, 17, 20
Shoulder stretch, 48
Singlets, 20
Sleep patterns, 155
Smoking, 28
Socks, 16
Speed for workouts. *See also* Pace for
    workouts
    categories of, 9-11
    for specific zones, 56, 80, 115
    techniques for measuring, 53
Speed play walks
    definition and guidelines, 80, 103
    orange zone, 105-109
    purple zone, 87-90
    treadmill, 90
    yellow zone, 97
Stationary exercise equipment, 149. *See also*
    Treadmill walks
Steady walks
    blue zone, 72-75
    definition and guidelines, 56
    green zone, 62-65
    purple zone, 81-83
    treadmill, 66, 78
    yellow zone, 93-94
Stereo headsets, 18, 24

Stereo headsets, 18, 24
Strength
    benefits of walking for, 5-6
    exercises for, 6, 151-152
Stretching exercises
    basic guidelines, 42, 43
    basis of need for, 5, 151
    specific exercise instructions, 43-48
Stride length, 35
Strolling, definition of, 9
Summer walking, 22
Sunglasses, 18
Sweatsuits, 17
Swimming, 148-149

T
Target heart rate, 50-51. *See also* Intensity of
    workouts
Technique for walking, 33-39
Tempo walks. *See also* Challenge tempo
        walks
    definition and guidelines, 79
    orange zone, 109
    purple zone, 84-86
    red zone, 123, 126, 127
    treadmill, 90, 127
    yellow zone, 95-96
Ten kilometer (10K) races, 122, 124, 125
Ten percent (10%) rule, 132
Threshold interval walks, 116, 118-119
Tights, 20
Time for workouts. *See* Duration of workouts
Tops (clothing), 17, 20
Tracks, walking on, 53
Traffic safety, 18, 23-24
Training schedules. *See* Programs for walking;
        Schedules for walking
Treadmill walks
    basic guidelines, 144-145
    blue zone, 78
    challenge tempo, 114
    green zone, 66
    long, 102
    orange zone, 114
    purple zone, 90
    red zone, 119, 127
    speed play-tempo, 90
    steady, 66, 78
    tempo, 90, 127
    threshold intervals, 119
    yellow zone, 102

Turnover, 35
Twelve kilometer (12K) races, 125
Twenty kilometer races, 126

U
Upper body, and walking technique, 35-37,
        38, 39
USA Track & Field, 4, 115

V
VO$_2$max (maximal oxygen uptake), 30-31

W
Waist lean, 38
Walkers, statistics on, 3-4
Walking Magazine, The, 4, 5, 15
Walking programs. *See* Programs for
        walking
Walks, types of, 55-56, 67-68, 79-80,
        103-104, 116
Warming up, 41-42, 53
Watches, 18, 20
Weather, 21-23
Weatherproof clothing, 18, 20
Weight, body
    for evaluating progress, 154
    fitness assessment of, 27
Weights, hand, 18
Wind-chill, 23
Winter walking, 21, 23
Workout zones
    basic guidelines, 53
    blue zone, 67-78
    caloric costs table, 52
    color-coding explained, 49-50
    green zone, 55-66
    intensity table, 50
    orange zone, 103-114
    for program selection, 130
    purple zone, 79-90
    red zone, 115-127
    types of walks in, 55-56, 67-68, 79-80,
        103-104, 116
    yellow zone, 91-102

Y
Yellow zone workouts
    basic guidelines, 91-92
    preview, 92
    specific instructions, 93-102

About
the Author

Therese Iknoian is one of America's leading authorities on fitness walking. She is involved in the activity in a number of capacities: walking instructor, journalist writing on the subject, and competitive race walker.

Therese has worked as a walking instructor for nearly a decade and has represented such companies as Rockport and Side 1. She was also the developer and instructor for Nike Inc.'s RunWalk program. As a free-lance writer specializing in health and fitness, Therese has had her articles published in such magazines as *American Health, Self, Men's Fitness, The Walking Magazine*, and *Women's Sports and Fitness*. In addition, she has written a syndicated sports and fitness column since 1992. Therese is also a nationally ranked race walker who has won numerous awards, including two silver medals at the 1993 and 1994 National Masters Track & Field Championships. In 1994, she broke the world record for her age group in the indoor 3-kilometer race walk.

Therese is a certified instructor for the American Council on Exercise and is certified by the American College of Sports Medicine as a health/ fitness instructor. She is a member of IDEA—The International Association of Fitness Professionals—and she is a featured presenter at their conventions. Therese lives in San Jose, CA, where in her free time she enjoys reading, cooking healthy foods, and playing with her German Shepherd, Chaco.